Foul Deeds & Suspicious Dea

The Black Country

DAVID J COX AND MICHAEL PEARSON

Published in association with the
Black Country Society

Series Editor
Brian Elliott

Wharncliffe Books

First Published in Great Britain in 2006 by
Wharncliffe Books
an imprint of
Pen and Sword Books Ltd
47 Church Street
Barnsley
South Yorkshire
S70 2AS

Copyright © David J Cox and Michael Pearson 2006

ISBN: 1845630041

Typeset in 11/13pt Plantin by Concept, Huddersfield.

Printed and bound in England by
CPI UK.

Pen and Sword Books Ltd incorporates the Imprints of
Pen & Sword Aviation, Pen & Sword Maritime,
Pen & Sword Military, Wharncliffe Books,
Pen & Sword Select, Pen and Sword Military Classics
and Leo Cooper.

For a complete list of Pen & Sword titles please contact
PEN & SWORD BOOKS LIMITED
47 Church Street
Barnsley
South Yorkshire
S70 2BR
England
E-mail: enquiries@pen-and-sword.co.uk
Website: www.pen-and-sword.co.uk

Contents

Acknowledgements

We would like to acknowledge the help and assistance given by the numerous archives, libraries and record offices visited during the course of our research. Special thanks must go to the Black Country Society, University of Birmingham Library, Keele University Library, Dudley Local History and Archives Centre, the *Express & Star*, the *Black Country Bugle*, Wolverhampton Archives, Lord Cobham of Hagley Hall for allowing access to his land, and The National Archives, Kew.

Michael Pearson would like to thank his wife Linda for her typing and patience when accompanying him on site visits. David Cox would like to record his appreciation of his father Frank Cox's assistance with material relating to the Gunpowder Plot.

The majority of photographic illustrations in the book have been taken by the authors. Due permission has been sought and sources credited for those other illustrations that are copyrighted.

The Black Country Society

This voluntary society was founded in 1967 as a reaction to the trends of the late 1950s and early 1960s. This was a time when the reorganisation of local government was seen as a threat to the identity of individual communities and when, in the name of progress and modernisation, the industrial heritage of the Black Country was in danger of being swept away. The general aims of the Society are to stimulate interest in the past, present and future of the Black Country and, wherever possible, to encourage and facilitate the preservation of the Black Country's heritage.

The Society, which now has over 2,500 members worldwide, organises a yearly programme of activities. There are five venues in the Black Country where evening meetings are held on a monthly basis from September to April. In the summer months, on a fortnightly basis, there are guided evening walks in the Black Country and its green borderland and there is also a full programme of excursions further afield by car and by coach. From time to time the Society publishes material by Black Country writers and researchers on subjects ranging from humour to industrial archaeology.

Details of all these activities are to be found on the Society's web site www.blackcountrysociety.co.uk and in the Society's quarterly magazine, *The Blackcountryman*.

For membership details, please contact:

The Membership Secretary
25 Foxhills Park
Netherton
Dudley
West Midlands
DY2 0JQ

Christopher Saxton's map of Staffordshire showing the Black Country, 1579. The Black Country covers an area of some 150 square miles, bordered by Wolverhampton, West Bromwich, Halesowen and Stourbridge. The term 'Black Country' was first used in the mid-nineteenth century and refers to the preponderance of coal-mining and heavy industry in the area. Authors' collection

Introduction

Crime has always exerted a fascination over us and it continues to do so: witness the often-lurid headlines to be found in every newspaper or the plethora of detective stories and radio or television programmes, both factual and fictional, that we avidly devour.

This book contains a wide variety of suspicious deaths and foul deeds that have a Black Country connection over a 600-year period from the Middle Ages through to the middle of the twentieth century. Within its pages can be found all the elements of criminality that so intrigue us: murder, violence, bad behaviour, detection, punishment, and even in some cases, a sneaking admiration for a likeable or outrageous rogue.

Each generation seems inclined to hark back to a mythical 'golden age', and this is certainly the case when discussing crime. Consider the following statements:

Highway robbery and burglary were common. It was not safe to go out after dark.

It was not safe to go out at night 'owing to the profusion of housebreakers, highwaymen, and footpads – and especially because of the savage barbarity of the two latter, who commit the most wanton cruelties.'

Either of these statements could have appeared in newspaper columns within the past few years, illustrating a perceived breakdown of law and order in contemporary society. In fact, the first was written about life in the 1840s by a Victorian poacher, James Hawker, whilst the second was penned in October 1751. Unfortunately no national crime statistics were kept before 1805, so it is impossible to compare accurately crime figures from the past with those that are reported today. However, as the following pages will show, crime was far from absent in and around the Black Country in the preceding centuries; and some of these, as illustrated in the book, could be extremely brutal and inhuman.

The object of this book is not merely to recite dramatic and fascinating cases of foul deeds and suspicious death – to do so would involve little more than regurgitating contemporary newspaper reports of trials. Instead, whilst hopefully engaging readers' attention with sixteen different cases, we have sought to relate these cases to wider developments in criminal justice history. Several of the cases illustrate particular aspects of crime, detection or punishment: the absence of what we would now recognize as a police force, the difficulty of proving the identity of a murderer due to the limitations of forensic science, the different ways in which men and women were treated before the law, and the often brutal forms of punishment that were meted out to criminals.

The book has therefore been conscientiously and meticu-lously researched using a wide variety of primary and secondary sources in order to provide a cross-section of foul deeds and suspicious deaths from around the Black Country. It includes murders, impostures, fraud, high and petty treason, and atro-cious behaviour by the forces of law and order. The term Black Country is used in its widest sense and cases are included that occurred or originated outside the area, but which either were perpetrated by persons born in the Black Country, or where significant incidents pertinent to the crime took place in the area. Thus we have included an account of the final events of the Gunpowder Plot, which were played out in the Black Country, and also details of one of the most famous of all eighteenth-century criminals, Jonathan Wild, who was born in Wolverhampton, but committed the majority of his crimes in London.

Cases are also included in which the perpetrator remained undetected and in which the guilt of those condemned remains uncertain. The criminal justice system has changed almost beyond recognition in the past millennium, and this is reflected in cases being brought in the past which a present-day judge would undoubtedly throw out for lack of evidence or pre-trial prejudicing of the jury, resulting in what we would now term an 'unsafe conviction'.

We have endeavoured to give readers a flavour of crimes that have occurred in the past few centuries, and have hopefully chosen a wide cross-section of cases that will engage people's interest. We have also tried to show the human aspect of all the cases, as the people detailed in them existed and either suffered their fate or carried out often foul deeds in reality; these events actually happened and should not be seen merely as stories by which to frighten or entertain ourselves. Consequently no cases more recent than the middle of the twentieth century have been included in order to avoid any distress or discomfort to any relatives or friends of those involved.

Whilst we in Britain have been relatively fortunate in recent years in having developed a reasonably robust and fair legislature and judiciary, together with a democratically accountable police force, this has not always been the case. This book illustrates that many of the constituents forming the bedrock of our present criminal justice system, including the right to defend oneself before a jury, the right to a fair trial, the right to appeal after judgement, the existence of an efficient police force, the need for prosecutors to prove a defendant's guilt rather than a defendant prove his/her innocence, and the reliance on judges to be apolitical and impartial, are in fact relatively modern constructs, and that our predecessors could not count on many of these rights or developments.

We hope that readers enjoy the cases detailed in the following pages and that they are also stimulated to find out more about Britain's fascinating criminal justice history. A brief 'Further Reading' section is provided at the end of the book in order to point any readers who may be thus inspired in the right direction. Finally, although the most meticulous care has been taken to ensure the accuracy of facts and events detailed within the following pages, it must be appreciated that we are dealing with records of cases that stretch back over several centuries. There are consequently occasions in which different sources give different versions of events. Any errors or omissions that may have occurred as a result are therefore apologised for in advance.

A brief note on the English legal system
The English legal system, although subject to several changes throughout the centuries, has in essence remained remarkably

similar in its constitution. During the majority of the period covered by this book, criminal cases were first brought before a magistrate or justice of the peace at either Petty Sessions (which could occur as and when the need arose) or, for more serious cases, Quarter Sessions (which, as their name implies, were held every quarter of the year). In cases where the magistrates felt that they were unqualified to deal with the complicated or extremely serious nature of the crime, defendants would be held in gaol to await trial at Assizes, which were presided over by State-appointed judges, and which usually took place twice a year in the county town – at Lent (March) and Summer (usually late-July). Winter Assizes could also be held if warranted by the number of cases waiting to be tried in any particular year.

Stocks and whipping-post used to punish petty offenders. The authors

CHAPTER 1

Juliana de Murdak: From Marriage to Murder 1316

This chapter illustrates how the mediaeval justice system functioned, following an extremely bloody and protracted murder of a husband by his wife. The perpetrator, a lady of noble birth, paid the ultimate price for her misdeeds whilst her co-accused, a knight of the realm, managed to escape her dreadful fate. The case is interesting not just because of its gruesome nature and singularly large number of conspirators, but in its illumination of how women were viewed and treated in mediaeval England.

On the night of Easter Monday 12 April 1316 a brutal and calculated murder took place at Stourton Castle, situated on the western fringes of the Black Country near Stourbridge. Sir Thomas de Murdak was staying at the castle with his wife, Juliana, and their retinue of servants. The constable or keeper of the castle was Sir John de Vaux, who had held the castle and the manor of nearby Kinver since December 1310, after exchanging the two areas for the hundred of Bradford in Shropshire with Walter de Kyngeshemede.

In a scene reminiscent of Shakespeare at his most bloodthirsty, Sir Thomas had retired to his bedchamber and was sleeping when he was first hit over the head with a staff by William, son of Richard de Bodekisham, a servant of Sir Thomas's. The unfortunate victim was then stabbed by Robert Ruggele, a seneschal (steward) of the Murdak household and Juliana's private chaplain, with a dagger up to the hilt – the blade apparently piercing right through Sir Thomas's body. He was then 'spitted above the navel' to his chest with a knife wielded by Roger de Chamberlain, another servant of Juliana's. The heinous crime was also apparently abetted by William Shene, a cook and Adam Palfreysman, a servant of the de Vaux household.

Apart from the fact that it appears that Sir Thomas was not a man who made friends easily, the gruesome murder was unusual in that it seemed to involve the majority of the household servants of both the de Vaux and Murdak households – three other servants of the Murdak family were also subsequently accused of complicity in events connected with the murder.

After the frenzied but obviously calculated and premeditated murder, Sir Thomas's head was severed from his body and his corpse dismembered. The body parts were then smuggled out of Stourton Castle and dumped in the grounds of Sir Thomas's manor of Edgecote in Northamptonshire, where they were discovered several days later. On 15 April 1316, only three days after the unfortunate demise of her first husband, Juliana travelled to Lichfield where she married Sir John de Vaux.

These are the bald facts of the murder of Sir Thomas, but despite almost seven centuries having passed since the foul deed, it is still possible to study contemporary documents in order to ascertain more details and background about the circumstances of the murder. This is thanks both to assiduous and dedicated mediaevalists, who have translated many of the surviving documents into English from mediaeval Latin, and the retentive nature of countless bureaucrats who simply refused to countenance throwing away any records in their care.

The Murdak family were a long-established and wealthy group of landed gentry, who had been granted lands at Compton Murdak (now Compton Verney) near Stratford-upon-Avon in the mid-twelfth century. Sir Thomas de Murdak had succeeded to the estate some time after 1298, following the death of his elder brother John. By this time Thomas was already apparently married to Juliana de Gayton, the daughter of Sir Philip de Gayton of Gayton, Northamptonshire.

Sir Philip may well have been a Crusader Knight, as his ornate tomb in St Mary the Virgin Church, Gayton, contains an oak effigy of a knight with crossed legs – usually an indication that the knight depicted had fought in a crusade.

Sir Philip died in 1316 at his manor of La Grave, Warwickshire on Tuesday, the feast of Saints Sebastian and Fabian (20 January), and his son and heir Theobald died at the same location on Saturday 24 January. There is no explanation

The gatehouse at Stourton Castle, near Stourbridge. The authors

in the records for the sudden death of the two men within a week of each other. It is known that the early decades of the fourteenth century saw several outbreaks of typhoid, dysentery and diphtheria, and it has been estimated that these three diseases accounted for the death of some ten per cent of the population. Whatever the reason behind their deaths, Juliana and her younger sister Scholastica (already a widow at the age of twenty-four) now inherited considerable land and property. An inquest held at Northampton on 1 March 1316, after the receipt of a writ of 7 February of the same year shows that Juliana and Scholastica were claiming the right to a rent of ten

The tomb of Scholastica de Meaux, sister of Juliana de Murdak, who died in 1354, after being widowed at the age of twenty-four. Scholastica's graceful and beautiful effigy may have been carved by William de Ireland, who also sculpted one of the Eleanor Crosses erected by Edward I following the death of his wife Eleanor of Castile in 1290. The authors

marks (a mark was worth 160 pence) from a burgage (plot of land within a town) that Philip had bequeathed to William, the parson of the church at Gayton. Eight days later, Juliana and Scholastica were involved in another dispute, this time over the ownership of the manor of La Grave in Warwickshire, which Philip had only held for life (i.e. not in perpetuity).

Juliana was by Easter 1316 a wealthy woman, having inherited half of her father's and brother's estate. However, English law at the time was not propitious to married women. Any goods or lands that a wife inherited during the course of her marriage became the property of her husband, who could exercise almost total control over them. The wife had no legal say in how her inherited lands were administered by her husband during the course of their marriage. Basically, the husband owned his wife. This law was based on Biblical tradition: St Paul's first epistle, Corinthians chapter 7, verse 39

Tomb of Sir Philip de Gayton (died 1316), St Mary the Virgin Church, Gayton, Northampton-shire. The authors

states that 'The wife is bound by law as long as her husband lives; but if her husband dies, she is at liberty to be married to whom she will', and this was the foundation for the legality of the husband's ownership of his wife and her property.

Whether this law provided the spark for Juliana's subsequent involvement in the brutal murder of her husband or whether she simply wanted to be rid of him will never be known, but she was undoubtedly implicated in the foul deed. The fact that she married so quickly after the death of her husband probably also helped to incriminate her in many people's eyes. Although Pope Innocent III had decreed in 1201 that widows could remarry at any time without suffering religious infamy, by the early fourteenth century it was a prescribed custom to undergo a period of a year's mourning.

An inquest was held on Wednesday 29 June 1316 at Warwick, in which Thomas's affairs were discussed, including the fate of Compton Murdak, which Guy de Bello Campo (Beauchamp), late Earl of Warwick had granted to Philip de Gayton, who in turn had willed it to Thomas. It was finally decided on 2 July that Thomas's son, John was the legal heir and the manor was subsequently officially delivered to him. There is some confusion as to John's age at the time of his father's death; other sources independently give Juliana's and Thomas's respective ages as twenty-six and twenty-eight, but the *Inquisition Post Mortem* held after Thomas's death specifically states that 'John his son (is) aged eighteen at the feast of St Bartholomew next'. Either both Juliana and Thomas were married whilst children, with Juliana giving birth at the age of nine (unlikely but not impossible, and this would tie in with other evidence that they were married by 1298), or there is a

Compton Verney, Warwickshire, site of the Compton Murdak estate owned by Sir Thomas de Murdak in the fourteenth century. The Murdaks were lords of the manor of Compton from the mid-twelfth century until 1370. The authors

St Mary the Virgin Parish Church, Gayton, where members of the Gayton family would have worshipped in the early fourteenth century. The authors

copying error in the *Inquisition Post Mortem*; perhaps John was eight rather than eighteen. However, the latter would suggest that John would have received his inheritance under the care of a legal guardian, and there is no mention in any of the sources that this was the case.

Despite the discovery of the dismembered body of Sir Thomas very shortly after it had been unceremoniously dumped at one of his estates in Edgecote, the full facts of the murder did not emerge for several years. Juliana and John de Vaux were not captured at once following the murder of her husband, and nothing appears in the official records until 30 September 1317 when Robert Ruggele turned his evidence at his trial for involvement in the murder of his master. It is not known how Ruggele was brought to trial, but in order to save his own life, he immediately implicated six other people in the murder, quite apart from himself and Juliana. The next record of the crime is found in the records of the Court of King's Bench held at Easter 1318, when the Sheriff of Warwickshire was ordered to arrest John de Murdak, son of William de Murdak (and probably the nephew of Thomas) for failing to follow through his prosecution of Juliana and several members of her household for the death of Thomas. Failure to proceed in such a prosecution could lead to a hefty fine and eventually outlawry.

There are no extant descriptions of Juliana but she seems to have exercised considerable fascination over both the Sheriffs of Staffordshire and Warwickshire. The Sheriff of Staffordshire was censured for sending a report to his counterpart in Warwickshire stating that Juliana was in his custody, when in fact he had let her go, whilst in 1320 the Sheriff of Warwickshire was accused of falsely returning false evidence in order to aid Juliana's case.

However, despite these attempts of help, Juliana was eventually committed for trial and was sent to the Marshalsea Prison in London on 4 October 1320 to await her appearance before a judge. Her conspirator and second husband, John de Vaux, was arrested shortly afterwards on 2 November 1320 in London and taken to the Tower. Juliana's trial for the crime of petty treason (rather than simple murder) was held on 20 January 1321 before a jury of twenty-four people, twelve of whom were knights of the realm. A 'Guilty' verdict was finally returned on 23 January (this suggests that there may have been considerable disagreement between the jury), and Juliana was sentenced to the ultimate penalty for petty treason: the Latin word '*COMBURENDA*' appears in the margin of the record of the verdict – 'she is to be burnt at the stake'.

In the event, there is some doubt as to whether this form of execution actually took place in Juliana's case. Although there are several such verdicts in the thirteenth and fourteenth centuries, only one woman is thought definitely to have undergone this painful death (in 1221 at Coventry). A record dated 16 November 1321 details the inquest into the late Juliana's land and property, and states that she was indeed burnt at the stake on 20 May 1321 for the murder of her husband, but another record dated 3 July 1322 proves contradictory, stating that she was instead hanged for the felony. She was found to have had goods and chattels to the value of £10 together with landed interests to the value of £130.

John de Vaux was somewhat more fortunate than Juliana. On the same day as she was sentenced, he was found guilty of bigamy. This was because John had claimed Benefit of Clergy upon his arrest. This was a legal loophole by which anyone who could read (or recite) Psalm 51, *Miserere mei, Deus, secundum misericordia tuam* [O God, have mercy upon me according to your heartfelt mercifulness] could claim to be tried by an ecclesiastical court rather than by secular royally-appointed judges. Benefit of Clergy was not withdrawn from those facing murder charges until 1512 by Henry VIII. Ecclesiastical courts were less severe in their sentencing and John was obviously hoping to escape a sentence of death. However, by marrying Juliana, he had committed the sin of bigamy, as common clerics were not allowed to marry widows. He spent several years in the Tower of London until being acquitted of all charges and released in 1325, finally dying around 1329.

It is not clear why he managed to escape the death sentence, as he was clearly implicated in the murder of Sir Thomas. The fate of the servants involved in the murder and its aftermath is also unknown, but it appears that at least two, Roger de Chamberlain and William Shene, also escaped serious penalty,

Woodcut of woman being burnt at the stake. Authors' collection

as in 1329 they are listed as having joined John de Vaux's household after the execution of their former mistress Juliana.

The motive for the murder seems to have been a combination of greed, love and hatred for her husband; his murder was particularly cruel and calculating, and her almost immediate marriage to John de Vaux only seventy-two hours after her husband's death suggests that they were extremely keen to be together. Her subsequent fate demonstrates that in mediaeval England, there was one law for men and another for women. There was no legal way out of an unhappy marriage for women such as Juliana, and although she obviously chose an extremely drastic and bloodthirsty way of ending the marriage, many women in similar situations must have suffered in silence.

CHAPTER 2

'We Mean Here to Die': The Last Stand of the Gunpowder Plotters 1605

This chapter demonstrates that terrorism is not simply a modern phenomenon: the Gunpowder Plot remains one of the best-known attempts to undemocratically upset the political status quo of the country. There has been much written about the Gunpowder Plot and the individual characters that were involved, but the extent to which the Black Country and surrounding area featured in the days and weeks after Guido Fawkes was caught red-handed under the Houses of Parliament on the evening of 4/5 November 1605 is not generally commented upon.

Whilst of course the main focus of attention concerning the Gunpowder Plot is London and ultimately the Houses of Parliament, much of the planning and recruitment of personnel involved took place in the West Midlands, mainly Warwickshire, Staffordshire and Worcestershire. In these areas together with many others, there existed strong sympathy and support for the Catholic cause. Principal Midland locations with connections to the Plot were: Coughton Court near Stratford on Avon, Hagley House near Stourbridge, Huddington Court near Droitwich, Hewell Grange near Worcester, and Holbeache House, Kingswinford, where the majority of the fleeing plotters were killed or captured.

In 1603 the Protestant Queen Elizabeth I died leaving no appointed heir. Eventually, James VI of Scotland accepted the offer of the throne. In so doing, he became James VI of England. Whilst James was a Protestant, Catholics in England had been led to believe that he would be a more tolerant monarch towards their faith than ever Elizabeth had been. They were to be sadly disappointed.

Holbeache House, near Kingswinford, Staffordshire. The façade of the house still bears witness to the Gunpowder Plotters' last stand, with musket ball holes in the brickwork. The authors

Since King Henry VIII's split with the Pope and the Roman Catholic Church over his divorce of his first wife Catherine of Aragon, Catholics in England had been subjected to religious discrimination and often fierce persecution. Heavy fines and sometimes imprisonment were imposed on anyone found to have been practising the Catholic faith. These penalties, together with the barring of any Catholic from the holding of any public office had been the order of the day under the respective rule of Henry and his Protestant daughter Elizabeth. It soon became apparent that James VI had no intention of redressing the Catholic grievances, and the festering unrest of the Catholic community was fast coming to a head.

The initial proponent and planner of the Gunpowder Plot was Robert Catesby, born near Lapworth in Warwickshire. Catesby brought together several like-minded Catholics to discuss his plan for the killing and overthrow of James I and his government which would be replaced by personnel more in sympathy with the Catholic faith. The main plotters were: Robert Catesby, Guido (Guy) Fawkes, Thomas Winter, Robert Winter, John Wright, Christopher Wright, Thomas Percy,

A contemporary engraving (attributed to Crispen van der Passe) of eight of the main conspirators in the Gunpowder Plot. Authors' collection

Everard Digby, John Grant, Ambrose Rookwood, Robert Keyes, Henry Morgan, Stephen Littleton, and Thomas Bates. Thus was the Gunpowder Plot conceived and measures to put the plot into operation were made.

The plot was of course discovered before one of the plotters, Guido Fawkes, could ignite the supply of gunpowder that had been transported in thirty-six barrels and stored in one of the cellars under the Houses of Parliament. After the capture and arrest of Fawkes, he was charged, tortured on the rack and after many days finally confessed, literally a broken man. After a show trial he was publicly hanged, drawn, and quartered on 31 January 1606 in the yard of the Old Palace at Westminster. Once his fellow conspirators realised that the plot had been discovered, they hastily left London and made their way to the Midlands to seek sanctuary and support from sympathetic fellow Catholics in the region.

Arriving at Warwick Castle, they raided the stables for fresh horses. From Warwick they travelled via Norbrook, Snitterfield and Alcester. On the evening of 6 November they arrived at Huddington Court near Droitwich, the home of the Winters. Here they loaded up carts with gunpowder, armour and guns.

The following morning, 7 November, they started out with the intention of making for Wales in order to seek safety and support. En-route they stopped at Hewell Grange in Worcestershire, the home of Lord Windsor, who was a kinsman of the Winters. Here, they stocked up with more supplies before travelling through Burcot, Clent, Hagley, and Stourbridge. In doing so, they had to ford the River Stour, which at that time of the year was in heavy flood. During the crossing the gunpowder on the carts became extremely wet, the result of which were to have serious consequences later at Holbeache House.

Holbeache House was the home of Stephen Littleton, a strong supporter of the Catholic cause. The conspirators, now consisting of about twenty men, reached the house late on the evening of 7 November 1605. Early the following morning, Stephen Littleton and Thomas Winter left the house to try to enlist the support of other Catholics in the surrounding area. They had no success and upon their return to Holbeache, found that there had been an explosion caused by the igniting of the gunpowder that had been soaked after the River Stour crossing the previous day being laid out to dry in front of an open fire. It now seems somewhat ironic that several of the plotters were undone by the very substance that they had hoped would change the course of English history. Several of the plotters were badly injured by the explosion which caused

River Stour, Stourbridge, near where the plotters' gunpowder was soaked (the Stambermill Viaduct shown in the photograph was built in 1881). The authors

considerable damage to the interior of the house. In the aftermath of the explosion, Stephen Littleton and Robert Winter left Holbeache together to try and seek refuge and help from Stephen's uncle, Humphrey Littleton (known as Red Humphrey to distinguish him from a relation with the same forename, and in some sources described as Stephen's cousin) who lived at Hagley House near Stourbridge (the present Hagley Hall was built on the site of the House in 1756).

Meanwhile, after receiving information concerning the location of the plotters, the Sheriff of Worcester, Sir Richard Walsh, had gathered together a large body of heavily armed men (what was then known as a *posse comitatus* – a group of the people) and arrived at Holbeache at about 11 am on 8 November. The defenders inside the house consisted of some of the main plotters, namely Catesby, Percy, Rookwood, Thomas Winter, John Wright, Christopher Wright and various others. On seeing the large force of men gathered outside, Thomas Winter enquired of his colleagues what they intended to do. Back came the reply, 'We mean here to die'. The Sheriff demanded the surrender of the plotters and after they refused, he ordered his

The conspirators' last stand at Holbeache House. Ernest Crofts RA, 1892. Authors' collection

men to fire the house and to attack the occupants. The attacking force was heavily armed with muskets, swords and crossbows and in the ensuing battle Catesby, Percy, John Wright and Christopher Wright were all killed; Catesby and Percy being felled with a single fluke musket shot.

Thomas Winter, Ambrose Rookwood and John Grant were all captured on site, and subsequently taken to the Tower of London to be accused, tried, convicted and executed. Henry Morgan was apparently taken to Stafford and subsequently executed. The contemporary account of the trial in London gives graphic details of the ordeals that the Plotters were to endure at their execution:

> *First, after a Traitor hath had his just Trial, and is convicted and attainted, he shall have his Judgement to be drawn to the place of Execution from his Prison, as being not worthy any more to tread upon the Face of the Earth whereof he was made: Also for that he hath been retrograde to Nature, therefore is he drawn backward at a Horse-Tail. And whereas God hath made the Head of Man the highest and most supreme Part, as being his chief Grace and Ornament [...] he must be drawn with his Head declining downward, and lying so near the Ground as may be, being thought unfit to take benefit of the common Air. For which Cause also he shall be strangled, being hanged up by the Neck between Heaven and Earth, as deemed unworthy of both, or either; as likewise, that the Eyes of Men may behold, and their Hearts contemn him. Then he is to be cut down alive, and to have his Privy Parts cut off and burnt before his Face, as being unworthily begotten, and unfit to leave any Generation after him. His Bowels and inlay'd Parts taken out and burnt, who inwardly had conceived and harboured in his heart such horrible Treason. After, to have his Head cut off, which had imagined the Mischief. And lastly, his Body to be quartered, and the Quarters set up in some high and eminent Place, to the View and Detestation of Men, and to become a Prey for the Fowls of the Air. And this is a Reward due to Traitors, whose Hearts be hardened.*

The grisly executions were carried out on 30 and 31 January 1606.

Sir Everard Digby was soon captured, together with Thomas Bates, a short distance from Holbeache. In due course they were tried and executed for their part in the conspiracy. In the aftermath of the siege, the Sheriff of Worcester was heavily criticised on two counts. One was of cowardice; he was accused of apparently sheltering behind a convenient wall whilst his men attacked the house, whilst the second was that he allowed certain members of his force to rob and strip the dead plotters of their possessions, including silk stockings and boots.

Meanwhile, after leaving Holbeache, Stephen Littleton and Robert Winter were hiding in various outbuildings belonging to the Hagley House estate owned by Red Humphrey. A tenant farmer of Rowley Hall and another servant were bribed to secrete and feed them. There is some debate about the exact details of this subterfuge, but two men from Rowley, Thomas Smart and John Holyhead (also recorded as Hollinshead), were subsequently charged with harbouring and sheltering the plotters and both were tried at Wolverhampton in January 1606 by a judge who was apparently brought over from Ludlow. They were found guilty and were hanged on High Green (now Queen Square), Wolverhampton.

Stephen Littleton and Robert Winter were then taken to Hagley House itself, where they hid for several days. They were finally discovered and betrayed by Red Humphrey's cook, John Fynwood, who became suspicious of the amount of food being consumed. They were captured and held at Stourbridge Gaol before being taken to the Tower of London where they were tried and executed. Red Humphrey himself having initially escaped to nearby Prestwood House in Staffordshire (owned by a relative, John Littleton), was captured, arrested and taken to Stafford Gaol then to Worcester Gaol. He was finally executed at Redhill, near Worcester on 7 April 1606, together with John Winter.

The wives of several of the Plotters were ensconced at Coughton Court, owned since 1409 by the Throckmortons, a prominent Catholic family. Everard Digby had arranged with the owner Thomas Throckmorton for the women to be lodged there whilst the events of the Gunpowder Plot unfolded. Throckmorton, whose family had suffered many brushes with

Coughton Court, Warwickshire, where the wives of several of the Gunpowder Plotters waited for news of their husbands. The authors

authority due to their recusancy, conveniently arranged to be absent from the house on the night that the Houses of Parliament were to have been blown up. On hearing that her husband and his co-conspirators had been captured, and that all was lost, Lady Mary Digby broke down in tears.

Thus ended probably the most famous foul deed ever witnessed in England. The Gunpowder Plot is still commemorated on Guy Fawkes Night (particularly in Lewes in Sussex, where an effigy of the Pope rather than Guy Fawkes is burned), and many people still know at least the first few lines of the subsequent doggerel that encapsulated the relief that the Plotters had failed:

> *Remember, remember the fifth of November,*
> *Gunpowder, treason and plot,*
> *I see no reason why gunpowder treason*

Should ever be forgot.
Guy Fawkes, Guy Fawkes,
'twas his intent
To blow up the King and the Parliament.
Three score barrels of powder below,
Poor old England to overthrow:
By God's providence he was catch'd
With a dark lantern and burning match.
Holloa boys, holloa boys, make the bells ring.
Holloa boys, holloa boys, God save the King!
Hip hip hoorah!
A penny loaf to feed the Pope.
A farthing o' cheese to choke him.
A pint of beer to rinse it down.
A faggot of sticks to burn him.
Burn him in a tub of tar.
Burn him like a blazing star.
Burn his body from his head.
Then we'll say ol' Pope is dead.
Hip hip hoorah!
Hip hip hoorah!

The anti-Catholic sentiment expressed in the song was undoubtedly fuelled by the discovery of the Plot, and it was many years before Catholics achieved equal legal status with Protestants in English law; the Corporation Act of 1661 and the Test Act of 1673 had banned Catholics from holding public office, and these were not fully repealed until the Roman Catholic Relief Act of 1829. To this day, due to the Act of Settlement of 1701, it is not possible for the Sovereign to either be, or to marry a Catholic.

There have been numerous theories as to the extent to which the Government of the day actually knew about the Plot before Guy Fawkes was arrested in the cellars of the Houses of Parliament. The Plot remains a subject for considerable historical debate. The 'Monteagle Letter', in which a member of the House of Lords, Henry Parker, Lord Monteagle, was warned not to attend Parliament has in particular caused many historians to doubt that Guy Fawkes' red-handed capture was

Queen Square (formerly High Green), Wolverhampton, site of the execution of two associates of the Gunpowder Plotters. The authors

just good fortune. Monteagle was married to Robert Catesby's cousin Elizabeth Tresham, and he received the letter on 26 October 1605. By his own account he immediately took it to James Ist's spymaster Robert Cecil, the Earl of Salisbury, who in turn showed it to the king on 1 November. However, the Houses of Parliament were not searched for several days, suggesting that the Government was already aware of a plot. Monteagle received a pension of £500 per year for his trouble, but it now thought that the letter was probably a forgery. Text of the Monteagle letter reads:

> *My lord out of the love I beare to some of youere frends I have a caer of youer preseruacion therfor I would advyse yowe as yowe tender youer lyf to devys some excuse to shift of youer attendance at this parleament for god and man hath concurred to punishe the wickednes of this tyme and think not slightlye of this advertisment but retyre youre self into youre contri wheare*

Prestwood House, site of Red Humphrey's capture following his involvement in the Gunpowder Plot. The authors

yowe may expect the event in safti for thowghe theare be no appearance of anni stir yet I saye they shall receyve a terrible blowe this parleament and yet they shall not seie who hurts them this cowncel is not to be contemned because it may do yowe good and can do yowe no harme for the dangere is passed as soon as yowe have burnt the letter and I hope god will give yowe the grace to mak good use of it to whose holy proteccion I comend yowe.

Whatever intricacies remain to be teased out by future historians, it is clear that the Black Country and the West Midlands played an important part in the foul deeds of the Gunpowder Plot.

CHAPTER 3

Wolverhampton's Thief-taker General of England and Ireland: The Foul Deeds and Death of Jonathan Wild 1683–1725

This chapter highlights the career and Black Country connections of one of the eighteenth-century's most famous criminals, and also illustrates the atrocious state of English criminal law and justice during the period. Wild's fate also demonstrates the hypocrisy of the legal system of the time.

Although Jonathan Wild was one of the most infamous villains of the eighteenth century, little is known of his early life. He is known to have been baptised at St Peter's Church in Wolverhampton on 6 May 1683, suggesting that he was also born in that year, as infants were commonly christened within the first few months of life to ensure that they would be received within the Christian faith should they die in infancy.

He was the eldest of five children, having two brothers (John and Andrew) and two sisters. John became a bailiff and Town Crier of Wolverhampton, where he achieved a brief notoriety in 1715 by disgracing himself by taking part in a religious riot. He died in 1720. Jonathan's other brother, Andrew, emulated him to a certain extent, following a life of petty crime.

Jonathan's father John was a joiner by trade, whilst his mother sold fruit in Wolverhampton Market. It is likely that Jonathan had at least a rudimentary education at the Free School in St John's Lane, but from his surviving letters it is clear that he occasionally struggled with the written word.

St Peter's Collegiate Church, Wolverhampton, where Jonathan Wild was christened in 1683. The authors

Little more is known of Jonathan's life in Wolverhampton apart from the facts that he married a local girl (possibly in 1703 as there is an entry for the marriage of a John Wild in the parish register of St Peter's, although this could refer to his younger brother), that he fathered a son, and that he became an apprentice buckle-maker. At the time Wolverhampton was one of the most prominent areas for the production of steel buckles for shoes. Such buckles seem to have become popular from the mid-1600s, replacing laces or strings. Jonathan apparently completed his apprenticeship, but in his early twenties he seems to have determined that this career was not for him.

The exact date and reason for his leaving Wolverhampton remains unclear, but by c.1704 he had deserted his wife and child and was living in London. It is uncertain whether or not he continued his trade of buckle-making in London, but by 1710 he had begun a downward spiral, being imprisoned for debt in Wood Street Compter (where Charles Dickens' father John was also later to spend some time). Wild spent a total of four years in the Compter, where he met Mary Milliner, a prostitute and petty thief, who was to play a significant role in Wild's subsequent life.

Wild was extremely fortunate in that in April 1712 an Act of Parliament was passed ('An Act for the Relief of Insolvent Debtors, by obliging their Creditors to accept the utmost Satisfaction they are capable to make, and restoring them to their Liberty'), which granted a discharge to any debtors who could prove that they could not meet their debts whilst imprisoned. Wild was duly discharged in December 1712 and he took up residence with Mary in a brothel in Lewkenor's Lane, Covent Garden (memorably described as a 'rendezvous for robbers and ruffians').

It was here that Wild learned the crafts of his new profession. He was firstly instructed by Mary in the art of 'buttock and twang' – a prostitute (buttock) would distract the attention of a client in order for her accomplice (twang) to divest him of his wallet, money or other possessions. He was also taken under the wing of Charles Hitchen, an under-marshal of Newgate Gaol and a notorious thief-taker and receiver of stolen goods. Wild soon picked up the necessary skills of being a receiver and fence. However, Jonathan was not content for long to be merely a petty player in such nefarious activities; he was extremely ambitious and soon set himself up as a thief-taker, negotiating the return of stolen goods and being instrumental in sending thieves to gaol and often the gallows.

Thief-takers were individuals who operated privately without any official status or power – they attempted to capture suspected

Jonathan Wild (extreme left) and Charles Hitchen watch as the pocket of an unsuspecting man is picked by a prostitute. Eighteenth-century woodcut engraving. Authors' collection

criminals in order to claim any reward money on offer from either the State or private individuals. It was widely believed that many of them operated illegally by framing innocent people or enticing weak-willed persons to commit crimes for which they were then arrested, with the thief-taker claiming any reward that was on offer. The practice of thief-taking was not new to the early eighteenth century; a John Pulman had been labelled as such in a trial of 1609. However, Jonathan Wild was to take the occupation to new heights (or depths!).

From 1712 Wild honed the skills of thief-taking to a new art, and in 1714 he set himself up in an office near to the Old Bailey (the main criminal court of London). From here he controlled a considerable network of thieves and informers operating throughout the Metropolis. He played the extremely dangerous but profitable double game of acting as a receiver for stolen goods, and as the taker of thieves in order to claim the often substantial rewards available for their successful prosecution. Included in his list of numerous victims was a William Smith, who was a well-known criminal and one of the creditors who had been responsible for Wild's spell in Wood Street Compter. Wild was obviously a man who neither forgot nor forgave easily; in 1791 he managed to get Smith transported for seven years for theft. Smith escaped, but was recaptured by Wild and received a sentence of fourteen years transportation (which he never served, dying on the journey).

Receivers were not above the law; an Act of 1691 made a receiver an accessory after the fact and liable to whipping, branding and seven years' transportation (or any combination of these punishments). An Act of 1706 increased the sentence against convicted receivers to that of death, whilst an informer who successfully turned Queen's evidence in order to convict his accomplices received both a free Royal Pardon and a reward of £40 – a considerable sum of money in the early eighteenth century. However, Wild sidestepped these laws by cutting out the middleman (the receiver) and dealt directly with both the victim and thief. He made sure that he never personally handled stolen goods; instead he would place carefully worded advertisements in the London newspapers, stating that he knew the location of missing goods and offered to return them to their lawful owners for a price.

He became extremely wealthy, buying himself a country house and set his thief-taking on a business footing, employing a manager and clerks. He dealt with famous and aristocratic clients, including Daniel Defoe and the 1st Earl of Dartmouth, William Legge, who owned Sandwell Hall near West Bromwich. A letter dated 15 June 1724 to the Earl from Wild survives in which Wild refers to the recent loss of some important correspondence and offers to retrieve the missing items:

> *My Lord, I am informed by Mr Woolley's man that your Lordship has lost some things on the road. I humbly beg your Lordship will please to order me a particular of them by next post and I will use all diligence I can to service your Lordship to the utmost of my power and beg leave to subscribe your Lordship's most obedient and dutiful servant.*

Although the Earl seems to have responded favourably to this letter, it appears that his steward was a more worldly and suspicious individual; a second letter from Wild to the Earl, dated 11 August 1724 makes it clear that Wild was getting frustrated with the steward's attempts to thwart him:

To the Right Honourable The Lord Dartmouth of Sandall Hall [sic] in Staffordshire,

My Lord, some time ago your Lordship suggested that you had lost some writing, which I endeavoured to discover, and after the reward of ten guineas was published, they [the thieves] demanded 20 for themselves, which your steward proposed to pay in part, if he could see all the writings, which were considerably more than your Lordship at first seemed to note, and had your steward paid all the money down your Lordship undoubtedly would have had them [the letters] before him. I was upward of six pounds out of pocket, and I would still endeavour to procure them for your Lordship would you please to order any one else to me than your steward, he always making so many trifling and needless excuses and putting-off in paying the money and expenses I have been at [...]. Should your Lordship please to order your commands be supplied they shall be faithfully obeyed.

By 1717, the government appeared to be in a particular quandary concerning Wild's activities; they were afraid of his growing operations and passed an Act to prevent the receipt of rewards for the recovery of stolen goods, but they were also aware that his work did to a certain extent control criminality in London and provided a means for the recovery of missing property. In 1720 Wild was even consulted by a parliamentary commission about what to do to prevent the growth of crime. Not surprisingly, Wild suggested that the reward system should be increased, thus swelling his ever-growing fortune.

However, Wild finally grew over-confident in his powers, and perhaps even began to believe some of his own publicity. In 1724 he even petitioned the Aldermen of the City of London to make him a Freeman of the City because of his usefulness in reducing crime. However, in the same year he made the serious error of capturing the notorious and popular Cockney thief Jack Sheppard. This individual achieved lasting fame by escaping from the condemned cell of Newgate Prison not once but twice. Sheppard was eventually recaptured and put to death, but Wild's popularity took a nose-dive as a result of Sheppard's death. Wild had already had many close shaves with violence as a result of his convicting several ruthless and dangerous criminals; he is said to have had received as many as seventeen wounds of different types during his life, and he wore two protective silver plates on his head as a result of two serious fractures. He also narrowly escaped death after having his throat slashed by a condemned criminal whose conviction he had previously arranged .

In 1725 he was finally hoist by his own petard, when he was accused of stealing and subsequently receiving a reward of £10 for the return of forty yards of lace valued at £50. He defended himself energetically and succeeded in being acquitted of the theft. However, he was found guilty of the receipt of a reward from the recovery of the lace under the provisions of the aforementioned Act of 1717 (ironically the Act was informally known as Wild's Act).

In a desperate last-ditch attempt to escape the noose, Wild wrote to several influential figures that he had dealt with previously, imploring them to intervene on his behalf and save him from the gallows. One of those contacted was the Earl of Dartmouth, suggesting that Wild had succeeded in returning the missing documents. The letter survives and is dated 23 March 1725:

I do not doubt that your Lordship will be surprised at my presuming to write to you, but I cannot but hope your Lordship will pardon me in so doing, because I am compelled to seek protection, by the violent prosecution of some magistrates (whom I never offended) who have encouraged several notorious thieves to swear against me, and to qualify them to be legal evidence, have procured his Majesty's most gracious Pardon, for crimes for which they have been condemned. If your Lordship would be pleased to give me a letter to such person as you shall judge proper to hear and redress me, I am confident that the designs of my enemies will be frustrated and I thereby at liberty to discover, apprehend and convict numbers of notorious criminals, which will be a great service to the public.

Jonathan Wild in his condemned cell at Newgate, 1725. Authors' collection

Contemporary satirical 'invitation' to the execution of Jonathan Wild at Tyburn, 1725. Authors' collection

Wild also published a list of over sixty criminals that he had convicted in an effort to swing public opinion behind his appeal for clemency; and also petitioned the King, but all such efforts proved fruitless. He was sentenced to be hanged on 24 May 1725. On the night prior to the scheduled execution Wild attempted to take his own life by taking laudanum. Unfortunately for him, he was not an experienced drug-taker and he misjudged the dosage, succeeding only in making himself semiconscious. In this state he was half-dragged from his cell and taken to Tyburn. He was unable to make a coherent final speech and the large crowd that had come to see the spectacle threatened to lynch the hangman when he attempted to allow Wild to prepare himself for his death.

Jonathan Wild may have been pleased to learn that he is still famous; after his death he was immortalised as the character Peachum in John Gay's *Beggar's Opera*, and was also the subject of a satirical biography by Henry Fielding, the author of *Tom Jones* and the creator of the Bow Street Runners. After his execution Wild's body was smuggled away to prevent it being stolen and it eventually ended up in the Hunterian museum of the Royal College of Surgeons in Lincoln's Inn Fields, London, where it remains to this day.

Wild certainly created a great deal of interest in the contemporary debate about law and order (or the lack of it) and is recorded in the *Proceedings of the Old Bailey* as being involved in almost forty criminal trials from 1716–24. He was undoubtedly a thoroughly reprehensible character, but to this day his irrepressible spirit and undoubted bravado ensures that he is remembered more as a likeable rogue than as a ruthless dealer in men's lives. His exploits also contributed to the growing call throughout the eighteenth century for a more effective system of policing and influenced many subsequent criminal justice reformers. We will see in the next chapter how policing, especially detective policing developed throughout the eighteenth and nineteenth centuries, with the advent of dedicated professional police forces such as the Bow Street Runners, created by Henry Fielding in the mid-eighteenth century.

CHAPTER 4

Bow Street Runners in the Black Country: The Arrest, Trial and Execution of 'Lord' Howe 1812–13

This chapter illustrates early nineteenth-century approaches to crime detection, justice and punishment. The cold-blooded and senseless murder of Benjamin Robins and the ultimate grisly fate of his attacker, William Howe, was something of a cause célèbre in 1812/13 – there was a considerable amount of newspaper coverage and vast crowds gathered to see both Howe's hanging at Stafford Gaol and his subsequent gibbeting at the scene of the crime at Dunsley near Kinver. However, a detailed study of the murder shows that there is much more of interest than simply a grisly and macabre tale.

Stourbridge in 1812 was a burgeoning small town on the south-western edge of the Black Country, with a population of around 4,000. It was already experiencing rapid growth and urbanisation, mainly due to the presence of glassmaking, coal and fireclay mining in the surrounding area. However, it was still predominantly agriculture that supported the local economy and society. The weekly Saturday market (known by 1812 as the 'Old Market', thus suggesting its long tradition; a market had existed in Stourbridge since at least the sixteenth century) drew a large number of prosperous farmers to its proceedings, and both contemporary and later evidence suggests that a considerable amount of financial transactions took place between such individuals and others within the town.

It was on such a Saturday market day – 18 December 1812 – that Benjamin Robins, a well-respected gentleman farmer who

Dunsley Hall, home of Mr Benjamin Robins. The authors

lived at Dunsley Hall near Kinver, carried out his particular business in the bustling town. Mr Robins was a popular and active member of the local gentry, with several respected friends, and from 1798 had been a member of the Stourbridge Local Volunteer Association of Cavalry, providing his own horse, uniform and weapons. Mr Robins, perhaps mindful of the cost of the forthcoming seasonal festivities that he was no doubt looking forward to sharing with his family, was carrying on his person two £10 notes from Messrs Hill, the Old Bank, Stourbridge; a £1 note from a Dudley bank, and 8s in silver. He left the town at around 4.30 pm, so that he should get home before the snow that had been falling throughout the day made travelling too difficult.

He set off on the relatively short journey along the unpaved but direct route to Dunsley via the Stourbridge–Bridgnorth road. At around 5 pm he heard a man's voice behind him requesting him to stop. Being somewhat short-sighted, in the failing light Mr Robins at first mistook the well-dressed man to be one of his brothers, Jeremiah. He consequently waited for the figure to catch up with him, to discover that the man was in fact a stranger who asked directions for the Kidderminster road. Mr Robins told him that they were not far from the required road (now the A449), and asked the stranger to accompany him as they were both going in the same direction.

This proved to be a fateful act of kindness: a contemporary account of what happened next is given in the *Staffordshire Advertiser* of Saturday 26 December 1812 (punctuation is original):

> *On Friday evening, about five o'clock, as Mr B. Robins of Dunsley, was returning from Stourbridge Market; he was over-taken by a man who walked and conversed with him for some distance; but when within less than half a mile of Mr Robins' house, the villain drew behind Mr Robins and discharged a pistol at him, the ball, it is supposed, struck Mr Robins on the back-bone, which caused it to take a direction round his ribs to near the belly; the place it entered, to where it was found, was from fourteen to sixteen inches. The villain, as soon as he had fired, demanded Mr Robins' money, who said, 'Why did you shoot me first? If you had asked me for it before, you should have had it.' Mr Robins then gave him two £10 notes, a £1 note, and 8s. in silver.*

The robber also demanded Mr Robins' silver watch, threatening to shoot him again with a companion pistol, before he ran off.

Mr Robins managed to stagger back to his home, where the alarm was immediately raised, and two surgeons sent for to attend his injuries. He managed to give a fairly detailed description of his attacker, and a handbill offering a reward of £100 above and beyond any statutory government-funded reward was hastily printed and also published in the local newspaper. Despite clinging to life for ten days, Mr Robins unfortunately succumbed to his wounds on the morning of 28 December, dying at the age of fifty-seven.

As the incident took place almost thirty years before Staffordshire gained a county police force, responsibility for the investigation of the crime fell on the local justices of the peace; in this case the magistrates who sat at nearby Stourbridge, and who would almost undoubtedly have known Mr Robins personally. By the early nineteenth century magistrates

Gibbet Lane, scene of the murderous attack on Benjamin Robins in 1812. The gibbet-post was allegedly removed in the late nineteenth century and was made into stile-posts for the nearby Prestwood Estate. The authors

were responsible for a wide range of public order duties and regulations, including the overseeing of criminal investigations (although it was extremely rare for the magistrates to involve themselves in the investigative process). Consequently the local parish constable, Mr Jones, was immediately given the task of investigating the unprovoked attack. He was certainly prompt in arresting two local men on the day of the attack, but this seems to have been more a case of rounding up the 'usual suspects' than a stroke of detective genius; both men were quickly released without charge.

The period during which the attack had taken place was a particularly unsettled one; mainland Europe had recently witnessed a cataclysmic revolution and Britain was subsequently in the middle of the Peninsular Wars, with the concomitant problems resulting from a long-term international conflict. The pages of many of the national newspapers of the time were taken up with lists of deserters who had either broken ranks abroad, or, perhaps of more immediate concern to the propertied and relatively well-heeled section of the populace who could afford to read of such events, those who had absconded from their barracks in England. The Luddite disorders were in full swing, and staple food prices were rapidly rising beyond the pockets of those most in need, leading to increased tensions in many areas.

During the early years of the first decade of the nineteenth century there had been sporadic riots throughout many parts of England, and Stourbridge was no exception. Indeed, Stourbridge had been the scene of riots in September 1766 as a result of the high cost of bread, butter and other staple foods. In 1800 there was a further series of disturbances among Stourbridge colliers due to the high cost of basic foodstuffs.

Threatening letters were also sent to those perceived to be profiteering from the scarcity of staple crops, and one such letter had in fact been recently received by Thomas Biggs, one of the Stourbridge magistrates:

> *Mr Bigges,*
> *Sir*
> *We right to let you no if you do not a medetley see that the bread is made cheper you may and all your nebern* [neighbouring] *farmers expect all your houses rickes barns all fiered and bournd down to the ground. You are a gestes* [justice] *and see all your felley cretyrs starved to death. Pray see for som alterreshon in a mounth or you shall see what shall be the matter.*

The attack on Robins undoubtedly unnerved many such members of the upper echelons of local society. As magistrates and farmers, the worthy justices of the peace at Stourbridge therefore had vested interests in ensuring that the perpetrator of the attack upon one of their fellow 'gentlemen farmers' was brought swiftly to justice. The worried Stourbridge magistrates, also conscious of the striking similarities of the attack on Mr Robins to the murder of another gentleman farmer, Mr Edward Wiggan, at Eardington, near Bridgnorth, on 25 November 1812, consequently decided that their local constable, no matter how eager, was not up to the job, and therefore decided to bring in the 'professionals'. They wrote a letter to London, requesting the services of one or more Bow Street 'Runner'. What Parish Constable Jones thought of this is unfortunately lost to posterity: perhaps he was relieved not to have had to chase an armed and ruthless individual, but on the other hand he may not have been happy at the possibility of missing out on a share of the considerable rewards on offer for the apprehension of Mr Robins' murderer. At this time there was no bar on official servants of the law sharing any proffered reward.

At the time of the murder of Mr Robins, there was considerable opposition to the creation of a state-controlled professional police force. In December 1811 the Earl of Dudley referred to calls for the creation of such a police force, following a series of particularly grisly murders in the infamous Ratcliffe Highway, London. He wrote to his sister:

> *They have an admirable police at Paris, but they pay for it dear enough. I had rather half a dozen peoples' throats be cut in Ratcliffe Highway every three or four years than be subject to domiciliary visits, spies, and all the rest of Fouché's contrivances* [Joseph Fouché was Napoleon's Minister of Police].

There was at the time no such force extant in England or Wales, though a paid full-time police force had existed in Dublin intermittently since 1786, and recent work has shed light upon the creation of pre-1829 police forces in several towns and cities in Scotland. Law enforcement was carried out by parish constables and watchmen at a strictly local level. What could perhaps be considered the only 'national' law-enforcement officers (in the respect that they were used throughout Great Britain) was the force based at Bow Street Public Office, where Henry Fielding, novelist and Chief Magistrate of Westminster, had created an embryonic police force of former parish constables between 1749 and 1753. By 1792 this force included eight Senior or Principal Officers, popularly known as Bow Street 'Runners', who operated solely as detectives.

The two Officers despatched to Stourbridge were amongst the most well-known and respected of the eight Officers employed by Bow Street Office at the time of the murder. Harry Adkins had been a witness to the assassination of Spencer Perceval earlier in 1812, and eventually became Governor of Warwick Gaol, whilst Samuel Taunton continued as an Officer until 1835. Adkins, in his evidence to a Parliamentary Select

Committee in 1816, stated that he had been employed at Bow Street since 1801.

Adkins and Taunton arrived in Stourbridge immediately after Christmas. Suspicion had by then fallen on a thirty-two-year-old journeyman carpenter living at Ombersley, William Howe, who had been seen by several witnesses in the vicinity at the time of the attack. Howe by all accounts was a bit of a 'dandy', with a preference for fancy clothes – he was apparently nicknamed 'Lord Howe' by his colleagues for his 'airs and graces' after his famous namesake, Sir William Howe, who had been Commander-in Chief of British forces during the American War of Independence.

An exhaustive investigation by the two diligent officers followed, involving travelling over 400 miles in pursuit of the suspect. Howe was found to have left his employ at Ombersley on 15 December 1812, and not returned until 22 December – he had then arranged for boxes containing his clothes and tools to be sent 'in the name of John Wood, to be left at the Castle and Falcon, Aldersgate Street, London, till called for'. The Bow Street Officers, through a combination of diligence and good fortune, traced these boxes (which contained a pistol and bullets), and lay in wait for Howe, who was subsequently arrested on 13 January 1813. He denied having been in Stourbridge, and refuted the charge that he had been involved in the attack upon Mr Robins. He was brought back to Stourbridge by Adkins and Taunton and was interviewed by Stourbridge magistrates on 19 January. He was transferred to Stafford Gaol on 26 January, where he awaited trial at the Lent Assizes in March 1813.

The inhabitants of Stourbridge seemed to have made up their mind of his culpability before Howe went to trial: the *Staffordshire Advertiser* of 6 February 1813 reported that 'A numerous meeting of persons resident in Stourbridge and the neighbourhood was held in Stourbridge last week, when £50 was collected for Adkins and Taunton, the Bow Street Officers, as a reward for their vigilance in apprehending Howe'.

Whilst in gaol, Howe made a desperate attempt to hide further evidence of his misdeeds – he asked another prisoner to pass a letter to Howe's wife via an intermediary, Elizabeth

Barlow. This illustrates that Howe was by no means a criminal genius, as unfortunately for Howe, his wife (whom he had only recently married – perhaps bigamously) was completely illiterate, and had to have the letter read out loud to her by a Mary Hodgson, one of the other residents at Mrs Vickers' lodging house, where Elizabeth Barlow was residing. The letter gave details of where a pistol, bullets and a bullet mould had been hidden in a hayrick near Oldswinford – this being either the murder weapon or its companion piece. Mr Vickers, the landlady's husband, read the letter after it had been given to him by Mary Hodgson, and immediately left for Stourbridge, where he informed Mr William Robins, a nephew of the victim. It is not recorded whether or not Vickers subsequently received a share of any reward. The letter had been given back to Mrs Howe, who apparently had sense enough to burn it to prevent its use as further evidence.

The pistol and bullets were duly found and later produced as evidence at Howe's trial. The trial took place at 8 am on 16 March 1813, under the jurisdiction of Justice Bayley, and lasted until 4.30 pm. Over thirty witnesses for the prosecution were called, and a compelling case was built up by Mr Jervis, the prosecuting counsel. The prisoner objected to one juror who was from the Stourbridge area (and who was subsequently replaced), but otherwise said nothing in his defence (at this time, the accused was not allowed to give evidence on oath). The jury took just seven minutes to find Howe guilty, and Justice Bayley sentenced him to death by hanging and subsequent dissection of his body for anatomical research. Howe apparently received the verdict impassively and 'appeared indifferent about his fate.'

Following the dictate of the 1752 Murder Act, the sentence had to be carried out within forty-eight hours of the verdict – there was no appeal procedure, and in this case, little chance of a Royal Pardon. (Incidentally Howe was probably hanged by Thomas Johnson, who was in 1816 himself found guilty of receiving stolen goods and sentenced to fourteen years' transportation). He apparently confessed to the murder at the gallows, declaring the 'badness of his heart', and went to his end 'with firmness and composure'.

100 POUNDS

REWARD

ROBBERY

AND ATTEMPT TO

MURDER

Whereas on Friday evening the 18th December, Instant, a little after five o'clock, as Mr Benjamin Robins, of *Dunsley*, in the Parish of *Kinfare*, in the County of Stafford, Farmer, was returning home from Stourbridge Market, he was accosted by a man near the end of Mr HILLS Park, who walked, and conversed, with him as they passed along the public road till they came upon Dunsley Hill, where the Man drew behind and immediately shot Mr Robins, in the back, and afterwards robbed him of two Ten Pound Notes of Messrs. Hill & Co. Stourbridge Old Bank, One Pound Note, of one of the Dudley Banks, Eight Shillings, and a Silver Watch. The Man who committed the above atrocious Acts, is about five Feet six or seven Inches high, appeared rather clean and well Dressed, having on a good Hat and a long dark coloured Coat, down to the calves of his Legs; his Legs a little bowed, and he seemed to walk wide – He was seen loitering about the Heath Gap, in the parish of Oldswinford, Worcestershire, some short time before the Robbery, and afterwards a Person answering to the above Description, was also seen returning along the same Road towards Oldswinford and Stourbridge.

Any Person, whether Accessory or not, who will give Information and Apprehend the above described offender, shall upon his Conviction receive a Reward of

100 POUNDS

to be paid by Mr ROBINS over and above what is allowed by Act of Parliament.

It is supposed that the above Offender called at some Public House in or near Oldswinford. Any information, however minute or circumstantial respecting him, will be gratefully received by Mr ROBINS or Mr Hunt, Solicitors in Stourbridge.

A reproduction of the printed handbill offering a reward of £100 for the conviction of Mr Robins' attacker. Authors' collection

It appears that the Stourbridge magistrates (possibly with the backing of Robins' family) were dissatisfied with the fate of Howe's body and successfully campaigned for the very unusual step of his body to be hung in chains (gibbeted) at the scene of the murder. This request was sanctioned by the Home Secretary, doubtless in an attempt to dissuade other would-be evil-doers. Anatomical dissection was the normal means of disposing of the body of a hanged person; a Christian burial was not permitted in the hope that the fear of not being allowed to rest in consecrated ground would also act as an added deterrent to those considering a serious criminal act.

The choice of gibbeting as a 'further terror' was not new to the eighteenth or nineteenth centuries; in his *History of English Criminal Law and it Administration*, Leon Radzinowicz states that 'according to the Rev. J. Charles Cox, the gibbeting or hanging in chains of bodies of executed offenders "was a coarse custom very generally prevalent in medieval England"'.

The reasons why this mediaeval 'custom' was still present in nineteenth century England are still the subject of discussion, but many historians hold the view expressed by Radzinowicz that:

> *Its purpose – like that of public executions – was to increase the deterrent effect of capital punishment; to achieve it, the process of executing the capital sentence was as it were, prolonged beyond the death of the delinquent.*

To this end, several measures were often taken to prevent the removal of the body from the gibbet, which was often a considerable structure; records show that Howe's gibbet cost £22 0s 0d. with the irons costing another £7 19s 6d. The gibbet was often of a considerable height (in Howe's case, it was apparently in excess of twenty feet high), and often studded with thousands of nails in order to prevent anyone from either cutting it down or climbing it to remove the body from the iron cage. Sir William Blackstone, a contemporary commentator on criminal justice remarked that 'the lower classes [...] have a great horror of the hanging in chains, and the shame of it is terrible for the relatives of the condemned'. Conversely, for the family of the victim(s), the gibbet could present a 'comforting sight to the relations and friends of the deceased'. It is interesting to note that the gibbet was constructed as near to the site of the murder as possible, but still out of sight of the Robins' family home, suggesting some sensitivity as to its siting.

Howe's body was therefore transported back to the scene of the crime at Fir Tree Hill, Dunsley, where a large iron and wood gibbet had been hastily constructed. The body was fixed to the gibbet by means of iron hooks being drilled into the bones of the cadaver.

Howe was one of the last men in England to be gibbeted – the last being James Cook in Leicestershire in 1832 – and various contemporaneous accounts tell of vast crowds flocking to see

Benjamin Robins' tomb, Enville Churchyard. The authors

the body, which was exhibited for a period of over twelve months. Estimates of the spectators vary from 20,000 to 100,000, but the macabre sight was certainly witnessed by huge numbers of visitors – day-long parties took place at the location of the gibbet. The name of the lane where the murder and subsequent gibbeting occurred was later changed to Gibbet Lane, being marked as such on the 1882 OS County Series map. As a gruesome postscript, accounts state that Mr Downing, the surgeon who had attended Mr Robins' wounds, returned to the gibbet over a year after the event and removed the bones, reconstructing the skeleton in his hall as a rather sick practical joke on his visitors. It was also reported that the decayed and dried flesh was left under a bush by Mr Downing, and was discovered by a pack of hunting dogs, but this is probably a lurid fictional addition to an already unpleasant tale.

No sign of the twenty-foot-high gibbet survives – it was allegedly made into stile posts for nearby Prestwood Hall. Gibbet Lane has turned into a rutted and little-used byway, but Dunsley Hall still survives as a well-maintained private residence. Benjamin Robins' grave is situated at the eastern end of Enville churchyard, from where one can look toward the area where his murder occurred. No allusion is made as to the reason for his unfortunate demise.

CHAPTER 5

The Suspicious Death of Sam Whitehouse 1822

Sam Whitehouse was a wealthy West Bromwich landowner with property in West Bromwich and elsewhere, including land and quarries at Rowley. He was related by marriage to Joe Downing, a farmer from Rowley (they had married two sisters). Sam was to meet his end on 5 April 1822, by violent means. We will explore the circumstances that led to his death and who, or what, might have been responsible for causing it. The incident became known as the 'The Halesowen Turnpike Murder' and led to the trial of Joseph Downing for wilful murder. The evidence of Sam's death was not conclusive, and murder was only one of a number of possible causes. The events of that day are well documented; there was a strong suspicion that he was murdered.

On 3 April 1822 Sam Whitehouse and Joe Downing had made arrangements to meet at the cottage of Thomas Fox, on the Halesowen to Birmingham Turnpike, opposite the junction with Beech Lane. The area at this time was a very rural part of the Manor of Halesowen. There was a little local industry, mainly nail-making.

Whitehouse and Downing were going to take part in a day's shooting in the nearby woods. Whitehouse arrived at the cottage at 8 am and was joined by Downing some two hours later. Downing brought with him the barrel of a gun and asked Fox to repair it for him. Fox was a blacksmith by trade and lent a fowling piece to Downing. The two men went into the woods to carry out some cock-shooting, leaving Fox to his work. They were gone for about five hours and returned at about 3 pm, they then left to view some property owned by Whitehouse, returning again at about 6 pm to join Fox.

The three men then took part in a bout of 'binge drinking', throughout the evening. Between then the men drank at least twelve quarts of ale. The men were in the mood to place bets with each other; the first was a £1 bet on the age of the Colt gun that Downing bought with him that morning. A much larger bet was discussed between Fox and Whitehouse, at one point Whitehouse pulled £10 from a roll of notes that he had in his possession. Fox however declined the bet and Whitehouse returned the notes to his left side breeches pocket.

More ale was consumed, with Downing plying Whitehouse by continually filling his tankard. By 9 pm. Fox's drunken visitors decided to set out for home. Downing was bound for his house in Rowley and Whitehouse for his West Bromwich home. Their route was shared for the first mile before they should have parted company at the Hill Top fork. The road was little more than a track through the woodland that was Little Lightwoods Park; they had to be helped onto their horses by Fox because of their intoxicated state. A few moments later Downing returned alone and asked Fox for the gun barrel he had brought with him for repair. Fox gave it to him, observing that Whitehouse had not waited for his companion.

An hour later Richard Aston, a resident at the *Beech Tree* tavern near to Fox's cottage, found a riderless horse wandering. Aston rode it towards Fox's cottage, knowing that Whitehouse and Downing had been drinking there earlier in the day (presumably because they had bought the ale from the *Beech Tree*). As he rode along the track Aston discovered Whitehouse lying on the ground, unconscious at the side of the track.

Aston rode straight to Fox to raise the alarm; Mrs Fox was unable to rouse her husband due to the amount of ale he had consumed. Mrs Fox rode with Aston to the location of the unconscious Whitehouse; also present was the smithy apprentice and between them they managed to take him to the *Beech Tree*. Whitehouse's money pocket flap was found to be open and it was empty. He was bleeding heavily from a head wound and was still unconscious.

At around midnight Fox was finally roused from his drunken stupor and informed of what had happened. He rode to Downing's house to inform him of the incident. Fox and

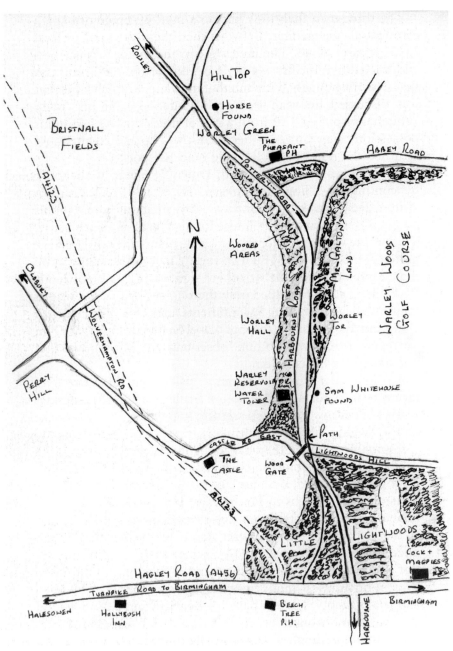

Map showing the Beech Tree *and turnpike, the location where Sam was discovered and other landmarks such as the* Pheasant *public house.* The authors

The spot where it is believed that Sam's badly injured body was found. Looking north, Warley Tor would have been about fifty yards away. The authors

Downing sat drinking mulled wine for the next two hours. Eventually Downing reached his badly injured brother-in-law, with Whitehouse apparently showing signs of regaining consciousness. Downing quickly left the injured man, stating that he wanted to search the spot where the incident had occurred.

The ride from the *Beech Tree* would take Downing through Little Lightwoods Park. The area in which Whitehouse was found was a footpath on the Warley Woods landscaped park. In the 1790s the land had been acquired by the Galton family. Samuel Galton, was a prominent Birmingham gun-maker and soon arranged for Humphrey Repton, a landscape gardener, to improve the estate. Repton developed Warley Tor, described in 1828 as a 'round building with a room right and left, of the simplest form for culinary purposes. A staircase led to a room above, from whence the scenery was viewed with greater effect'. There is now no trace left of the Tor, except on maps of the estate.

Whitehouse lived for two days and there were periods when he regained consciousness however, he was incoherent and most of his body was paralysed. He died on 5 April. The inquest into his death took place the following day at Halesowen, the following verdict was reached:

> *That Joseph Downing not having the fear of God, but being moved and seduced by the instigation of the Devil, did upon the person of the said Samuel Whitehouse, feloniously, wilfully and with malice aforethought, make an assault with a certain gun barrel made of iron and steel, to the value of ten shillings, which the said Joseph Downing held in his right hand and did hit, strike and beat in the hinder part of the head of the said Samuel Whitehouse, producing a mortal wound of the length of two inches and the breadth of half-an-inch, from which he languished and died on the said fifth of April.*

This verdict was read by Joseph Parsons, the jury foreman, and Downing was arrested by Joseph Grainger, the Halesowen constable and imprisoned to await trial at the Salop Summer Sessions. The judge at the trial at Shrewsbury was Sir John Bayley (the same judge that sentenced William Howe to death for the murder of Benjamin Robins in 1812); counsel appearing for the prosecution was Messrs Puller, Campbell and Male, and for the defence were Messrs Jervis, Pearson and Russell. Downing entered a plea of 'not guilty' stating he had not caught up with the victim on the night, nor did he see his body lying on the side of the woodland path, and claimed to know nothing about the tragedy until Fox came to his house to inform him of it.

Details put forward by the prosecution told that Whitehouse and Downing had married two sisters. Whitehouse had considerable wealth, owning a number of properties, he was childless and in his will he had left his estate to Downing's children.

One of the first witnesses to be called was Stephen West Bloxham, the Halesowen surgeon who had been called to treat Whitehouse's wound. He gave evidence that the wound could have been caused by the gun barrel that was shown to him. He denied a defence theory that the injury had been caused by kicks from a horse's hoof. The gun barrel theory was confirmed by the next witness, his father, Doctor Charles William Bloxham, also a surgeon at Halesowen. There was a conflict in the medical evidence, provided for by John Badley, a surgeon of great eminence from Dudley. His opinion was that the fatal injuries had been caused by the kick of a horse and not a gun barrel. Badley was the family doctor and had been called in by Downing to tend to Whitehouse. Downing had been unhappy with the treatment given by the Bloxhams.

Another witness called was Ezekiel Dearne, who lived in a cottage near Hill Top and helped Downing's case by stating that he had seen two strangers walking down the woodland track on the night of the incident. Samuel Hodgetts of Bristnall Fields said that the mare ridden by Whitehouse was skittish and, about a month earlier, had thrown Whitehouse and bolted. Whitehouse had called on Hodgetts to ask for help in catching his horse. The evidence about the horse was further substantiated by Thomas Bincks who was Whitehouse's servant. He said that the mare had an 'uncertain temper' and had thrown him about six weeks before the fatal incident. He had also seen the mare kick out in the stable 'enough to knock the door down'.

The prosecution made great play of the behaviour of the prisoner in the hours directly after Whitehouse had been found, pointing out how strange it was that Downing had chosen to 'dally over drinks' rather than go the aid of the injured man. They put forward a theory that the delay was to give Sam Whitehouse time to die, before being forced to confront him and possibly be accused of the crime.

Judge Bayley, once all the evidence had been given began his summing-up. The judge reminded the jury that they needed to be certain, within a reasonable degree, that the death was indeed murder, before considering any verdict against the prisoner. He also pointed out the evidence of the two strange men in the vicinity coming on foot from the direction where Whitehouse lay. He put before the jury the two possibilities to account for the fatal injury, refusing to give an opinion on whether this was at the hands of a human or the horse. On the missing money he pointed towards robbery by the two men. He concluded by making the statement;

> There is, gentlemen, abundant evidence from the circumstances of the case, to satisfy my mind that the prisoner could not have been that person.

Following such a strong summing-up in favour of the defence it came as no surprise when the jury returned a 'not guilty' verdict. The prisoner broke down in tears, and on the orders of the judge his irons were removed in the dock.

The trial was the talk of Rowley for many years and deeply affected the Downing family. None of Joe's four children ever married and all are buried in Rowley churchyard in the family vault. The last to die was son Isaac on 15 November 1874 when he was aged fifty-nine. The Whitehouse inheritance passed out of the hands of the Downing family; Isaac willing it on his death-bed to the son of the Reverend William Crump – vicar of Rowley from 1846 to 1858. The inheritance had included land and quarries at Rowley.

The location of the incident is now on the site of Warley Woods municipal golf course. The Halesowen to Birmingham turnpike roughly follows the route of the current Hagley Road. Fox's house would have been located about halfway between the junction of Wolverhampton Road (not in existence until the mid-twentieth century), and the *Cock and Magpies* public house (now a Harvester restaurant of the same name is to be found on the site of the old pub). 'Hill Top' does not relate to the place of that name in West Bromwich but the crest of the hill dissected by the Wolverhampton Road.

The nearest landmark to the scene is the Water Tower, erected in 1939, which remains today at the edge of the golf course. Shown on a map from the time is a castle, there is no trace of it, other than the fact that Castle Road East and West are divided by Wolverhampton Road. Another landmark I used to pinpoint the scene was a mention of the *Pheasant Inn* on an old map. There is still a pub with this name on the site of the original inn, not far from the scene of Whitehouse's demise. I believe the body was found, next to the path that runs alongside the second hole of Warley Woods Golf Course, somewhere close to the site of Warley Tor.

The *Beech Tree*, near to where Thomas Fox lived, and also the place where Whitehouse was taken after his injury, was almost certainly at the site of a current public house, the *Amber*

The Water Tower, the nearest modern landmark to the spot where Sam was found. The authors

Tavern. This is to be found at the junction of Wolverhampton Road and Hagley Road.

The question remains, how did Sam Whitehouse meet his death? It is clear that a blow to the head was the physical cause, but was this the result of foul play? His horse was allegedly very spirited and had thrown him on a previous occasion; there was also the evidence of his drunken state to consider. Medical opinion was divided as to whether the gun barrel caused the injury, a blow from a horse hoof was discounted, but could the injury have been caused by the fall itself? Another imponderable surrounds the roll of money in Sam's pocket. Robbery may well have been the motive for the attack; this would widen the list of suspects to include Joe Downing and the two mystery men seen by the witness Ezekial Dearne. The favourite suspect would be Downing, he knew of the money, and his family had much to gain by Sam's death. On the other hand, Sam would have been a prime target for robbers, the night was dark, he was very drunk and his clothing would probably have indicated his potential wealth. The money could also have been stolen after the injury was caused, by any number of suspects.

We will, of course, never know the truth, but a number of lives were altered by the death, whatever the cause; in particular the Downing family, who inherited Sam's fortune and lands, but do not appear to have benefited from their inheritance. The case remains a genuine mystery.

CHAPTER 6

A Quartern of Brandy, a Quartern of Gin ... and a Pinch of Arsenic? Poisoning at Rowley Regis 1838

This chapter demonstrates the extremely limited scope of forensic science available to the police in the mid-1800s. With the battery of sophisticated tests now open to current law enforcement agencies, the mystery of how the victim died would have been solved within days if not hours, instead of the events of the death unresolved.

On Wednesday, 11 July 1838 Samuel Perry, a forty-five-year-old nailer who lived with his wife Susannah and their three children in Garratt's Lane, Rowley Regis, woke at 5 am with terrible pains in his stomach. He had been feeling unwell on the previous day, when he had struggled to his nailshop at the rear of his property. He had, according to his wife, worked two pairs of irons and part of another (irons were the iron bars that the nailers fashioned into nails), and had made about 100 nails. This suggests that he had been far from well, as a good nailer could usually make as many as 3,000 nails per day. He had taken no food that day, and had drunk nothing but a quartern of brandy and a quartern of gin that had been given to him by his thirty-nine-year-old wife.

By Wednesday Samuel was feeling much weaker and was unable to rise from his bed. His wife said that she wanted to fetch a doctor, but Samuel would not hear of it. Doctors were very expensive (no National Health Service for another 110 years), and were also often mistrusted. As the day wore on, Samuel's illness progressed until he became extremely weak. Susannah began to panic and in desperation called in both her next-door-neighbour, Sarah Baker, and Samuel's mother, Rachel.

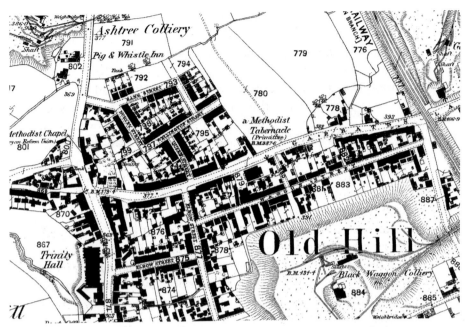

Garratt's Lane, Old Hill, Rowley Regis. First series OS map, c.1880. Authors' collection

Despite entreaties from both neighbour and mother, Samuel steadfastly refused to call in a doctor, stating 'I'll have no doctor here!', and telling his mother that the Lord would see him before any doctor did. This proved prophetic as he grew weaker and weaker, finally expiring at 1 am on Thursday morning.

On Friday 13 July, a constable from Rowley Regis, James Detheridge, was prevailed upon to visit Susannah, to inform her that there would have to be an inquest due to the sudden death of her husband.

Not surprisingly, it was decided that a post-mortem would have to be carried out; this was strongly objected to by Susannah, who seemed opposed to any form of dissection, but on Saturday 14 July a surgeon was called to the house in Garratt's Lane. The surgeon who carried out the post-mortem, which lasted four hours, was Samuel Day Fereday, who lived in nearby Dudley. Fereday was a local doctor of some repute, being a Fellow of the Royal College of Surgeons, and he was also a Justice of the Peace for Dudley. He was a few years later one of the surgeons and doctors who were interviewed for the

Children's Employment Commission of 1842. He seems to have had a very complacent view of the working and living conditions of miners, reporting that he thought colliers generally to be in better health than most of the population, and that apprentices to butties were well-looked after and treated.

Mr Fereday opened the stomach of the deceased and examined its contents in great detail. He found 'a quantity of white powder, opaque and gritty to the feel'. He conducted the limited tests then available to determine if arsenic was present in the body by boiling the white powder in distilled water and adding a solution of ammoniated sulphur of copper to one portion of the powder, and a solution of ammoniated nitrate of silver to another portion. Various tests had been developed since the late eighteenth century to detect traces of arsenic, but it was not until the mid-1830s that reliable tests such as the Marsh Test (developed by the eponymous James Marsh) were readily available to doctors (although Fereday does not seem to have tried this particular test).

The tests proved beyond doubt that Samuel Perry had died from arsenic poisoning. Arsenic had been known as a poison for centuries, and it is amazingly effective. One grain (65 milligrammes) is enough to kill an adult, and until 1851 it was readily available in Britain. In that year an Act of Parliament was passed, restricting the sale of arsenic-laced rat poison to persons over twenty-one years of age, who also had to be known to the seller and who had to sign a register. Arsenic had many uses, including the manufacture of glass where it prevented discolouration, and the treatment of syphilis. The majority of arsenic produced in England came from Morwellham Quay in Devon, where the stocks of the poison were said to be enough to poison every man, woman and child in the world.

Despite the post-mortem results, Susannah was not immediately arrested, instead being allowed to remain at home to look after her three children. The coroner's inquest was adjourned to 26 July as a result of the findings of the post-mortem.

Old Hill in the mid 1830s was a small close-knit community where everyone knew everyone else's business, and the rumour-mill went into overdrive over Samuel's demise.

Morwellham Quay, 1868. Courtesy of the Morwellham and Tamar Valley Trust

On the day of the inquest Constable Detheridge, along with Constable Joseph Jewkes, a member of the Dudley constabulary, conducted a search of the upstairs rooms and then searched the kitchen. He opened a corner-cupboard and found a small blue packet containing a white powder. He asked Susannah what was in the packet, and she stated that she thought that it was precipitate (a medicine). The constable pointed out that writing on the packet in fact pronounced it to be arsenic. Susannah then stated 'Then I did not know that', thus inferring that she was illiterate. This would not have been unusual; the *Manchester Guardian* of 25 April 1838 had reported that only just over fifty-two per cent of the population could read and write, and of this percentage, less than ten percent could read or write well.

The inquest was held before the Coroner, Henry Smith (the same coroner who had examined the body of Benjamin Robins some twenty-six years earlier). Mr Smith and the coroner's jury had no hesitation in pronouncing a verdict of 'Wilful Murder', and Susannah Perry was immediately arrested and committed to Stafford Gaol to await trial at the next Assizes.

Susannah was unfortunate in that she had to spend a considerable amount of time in Stafford Gaol, as the Assizes were only held twice-yearly; at Lent (March) and Summer (usually end of July). If there were too many cases to be heard at the two Assizes a third, Winter session could be held. However this was not the case in 1838 and consequently Susannah's trial was held over to the Lent 1839 Assizes. On Monday, 11 March 1839 she appeared before the judge at Stafford Assize Hall.

Susannah pleaded 'not guilty' to the charge of wilful murder and objected to one member of the jury, who was replaced. She was apparently distraught throughout the trial, fainting on two occasions. The jury heard that whilst it was not in doubt that Samuel Perry had died from arsenic poisoning, they were there to decide if Susannah was the guilty party. They heard evidence from James William Stanley Lawton, a surgeon and chemist of Rowley Regis that in the first week in June a young girl had come into his shop wishing to purchase some arsenic for her mother, whom she said wanted it to use in her business of cleaning straw bonnets. Lawton was not prepared to sell the poison to a child and told the girl to get her mother to call at his shop. A woman wearing a straw bonnet with blue ribbons attached to it duly called in and he sold her about a third of an ounce of arsenic. He examined the packet that Constable Detheridge had found in his search and confirmed that this was the same packet as that which he had sold to the woman.

Lawton believed that the woman was the same woman as the person standing in the dock, but he did admit that the straw bonnet which the purchaser of the arsenic wore did not appear to be the same hat as one found in Susannah Perry's house. A further complication to the trial was provided by several witnesses stating that they had seen the accused in close company with a James Smith, a nailer who was a friend of Samuels. The accused was apparently seen walking with Smith in Dudley on the evening of 10 July 'as though they were man and wife', and were also seen on the morning of 11 July in close conversation with each other.

The defence however mounted a strong case, pointing out that this was circumstantial evidence and that the accused had on several occasions tried to persuade her husband to see a doctor. She had also raised no objections to her house being searched, and, in what was probably the defining incident of the trial, the defence counsel pointed out that the search had not taken place until twelve days after the post-mortem had been carried out (no reason was given by the prosecution for this almost unbelievable delay in such basic police procedure). Such a delay would have given the accused plenty of time to dispose of any incriminating evidence.

Several character witnesses were called for the defence, including childhood friends and people who had known her for decades, and all stated that she had been an affectionate wife and a good mother. The judge conducted a lengthy summing-up, but this was not matched by the jury, who only retired for five minutes before returning with a 'Not Guilty' verdict. Susannah Perry was a free woman, but by this time was in such a state of insensibility that she had to be carried from the dock.

The above case illustrates that in the mid-nineteenth century murder investigations and trials were much simpler affairs than they have now become. The investigators of the day had extremely limited scientific resources to help them in their work. Fingerprinting was first successfully used to secure a con-viction in 1902, whilst DNA testing was not developed until the mid-1980s. Forensic scientist could not distinguish between animal and human blood until 1895, and this test was not accepted in a court of law until 1902. Quite apart from the lack of scientific techniques available to the investigators, the investigation seems to have been haphazard to say the least. The fact that the suspect was allowed to remain at large, and the failure to search the premises for almost a fortnight after the suspicious death seems extremely inept. No-one else was ever prosecuted for the poisoning of Samuel Perry, and the true circumstances in which he met his end remain a mystery.

CHAPTER 7

The Polygamous Life of 'Lord Kennedy' 1838–43

This case certainly qualifies under the heading of a 'foul deed', or perhaps more accurately, a series of 'foul deeds'. However, it also illustrates that the circumstances surrounding such deeds were not always devoid of humour. It can also be read as a warning against avarice (or hurried matrimony)!

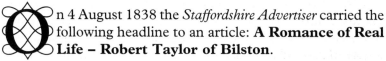n 4 August 1838 the *Staffordshire Advertiser* carried the following headline to an article: **A Romance of Real Life – Robert Taylor of Bilston**.

The article then detailed how a young man living in Bilston, Robert Taylor, had become the recipient of some remarkable good fortune. He was aged about seventeen or eighteen and had discovered that he was the illegitimate son of the late Lord Kennedy of Ashby Hall, near Asbhy-de-la-Zouche. The late Lord had apparently made an 'honest woman' of his mother some twelve months after their son's birth.

The son had subsequently been put to a wet-nurse in London, where the young Robert enjoyed a most favourable childhood until the age of about seven, when he was kidnapped by gypsies and eventually deposited on the parish of Bilston in the Black Country. The abandoned child was then apprenticed at the age of about nine to a collier's butty (a self-employed work-gang foreman who subcontracted employees for work in his gang). The child had been forced to work in a colliery and endure the harsh regime of an apprentice's life, until circumstances turned in his favour.

He was taken ill and a surgeon was sent for. The surgeon had previously read about the long-lost son of Lord Kennedy and was able to confirm his suspicions by looking at a birthmark on the child's right arm. The child was joyously reunited with his nurse, who was still alive in London, although the boy's mother had unfortunately died in the meantime. The child learned that as heir to the Kennedy fortune he was to inherit £1,015,000 in 3 per cent consols (Government stock securities, returning 3 per cent interest per annum), together with interests in coalmining, quarrying, shipping etc., which together would give him an annual income of £60,000. The inheritance would only come into force however after he married or reached the age of twenty-one.

The fortunate individual returned to Bilston after finding that due to the years of work in a Black Country colliery, he did not feel able to mix easily in polite society. He determined instead to find himself a local lass and settle down in the company of his Bilston friends. He was a deeply religious man and devoutly wished for a suitably demure and willing wife. He advertised that he would pay £10 to the person who could provide him with a suitable wife in the very near future. Not surprisingly, he was inundated with offers, but it appears to have been love at first sight when he was introduced to Sarah Ann Skidmore of Edmund Street, Birmingham by a hopeful relative of the putative bride-to-be. They were subsequently married at St Philip's Church in Birmingham on 28 July 1838, less than a week after they met.

The story as recounted in the *Staffordshire Advertiser* has all the hallmarks of a classic romantic tale; a long-lost son, an unexpected inheritance, and a romantic attachment.

Unfortunately, there is just one problem: scarcely a single word of Robert Taylor's rags to riches story was true!

Taylor was in fact a supremely confident confidence trickster, who inveigled girls to marry him, and who then systematically fleeced his new in-laws before deserting his bride. There was no late Lord Kennedy of Ashby Hall: indeed at the time there was no English lord with that title, although there was a Scottish clan leader, the Earl of Cassilis of Culzean Castle, who held the honorary title of Lord Kennedy.

The true beginnings of Robert Taylor were much more prosaic than the web of deceit that he spun gullible fortune-hunters. He was born in Fatfield, County Durham to Elizabeth

St Philip's Church, Birmingham, where one of 'Lord Kennedy's' numerous weddings was performed. The authors

Taylor, a single woman, and an undisclosed father. The family seems to have visited the Black Country in his early childhood and Robert was apprenticed at the age of nine to a collier's butty in Bilston. That much of the story was true.

The life of an apprentice collier was extremely tough and demanding, with little reward. The Children's Employment Commission of 1842 reported that:

> *Many boys and young men are working in the mines* [of South Staffordshire] *as apprentices. Such is the demand for children amongst the butties, that there are almost no boys in the Union Workhouses at Walsall, Wolverhampton, Dudley and Stourbridge.*

The boys were apprenticed as early as nine until they reached their twenty-first birthday. They received no wages (although some may have been lucky to receive 6d. weekly pocketmoney), and were fed, clothed and sheltered by the butty. One of the reporters to the Children's Employment Commission was shocked by the system, stating that 'Now here is slavery in the middle of England as reprehensible as ever was the slavery in the West Indies'.

Coalmining is documented as early as the fourteenth century in Bilston, and by the early nineteenth century it was very big business: the Parish Assessment Book of 1827 details twenty-five mine owners whose mines produced a total of almost 317,000 tons of coal. The coal in the South Staffordshire coalfield often lay in extremely thick layers; in certain areas the coal seam could be over thirty feet thick. The work in coal mines was harsh and conditions were generally appalling, with numerous accidents befalling colliers, especially apprentices who were not experienced in life underground. Understandably, Taylor was not too keen on this way of life and by the time he had reached the age of seventeen he had conceived a plan that would release him from his unending daily grind. Whether he forged the documents himself or whether he persuaded a more literate friend to create them is unclear, but he furnished himself with an impressive array of legal documents including a will from the mythical Lord Kennedy, an indenture 'proving' the validity of the will and numerous other items that reinforced

Bilston, with St Leonard's Church in the background. The authors

his story. These documents were carried around by Taylor in a metal tin with the name 'Lord Kennedy' written on it. In fact the receptacle was a collier's candle tin which was used to carry the candles necessary in a pre-electric age when working underground.

The next that readers of the *Staffordshire Advertiser* learned about the lucky 'Lord Kennedy' was on 9 May 1840, when the newspaper carried an article entitled 'Lord Kennedy Again'. The article recounts that Taylor, who had deserted his wife from Birmingham in a matter of weeks after acquiring as much cash from the gullible in-laws as possible, had turned up in Hetton-le-Hole in County Durham with a new wife, Mary Ann Davidson. The couple had taken their matrimonial vows at Aclam near Stockton on 4 April 1840, a day after Davidson had been presented to Taylor as a suitable candidate for marriage by her brother-in-law, the Reverend Benjamin Furber, a Methodist minister. The preacher had fallen hook, line and sinker for Taylor's tale, and was subsequently swindled out of £12. The married couple was seen walking on 5 April by Superintendent Inge of Durham County Police, who had been informed to be on the lookout for Taylor, who was thought to be in the area after bigamously marrying yet another young lady in Newcastle.

Superintendent Inge detained Taylor, who was dressed in a plain flannel coat over a collier's smock. The police officer learned through his subsequent investigations that Taylor had indeed married a Mary Ann Wilson, the young daughter of a Newcastle tobacconist on 19 October 1839. The marriage, unsurprisingly had not been a happy one, and Taylor deserted his new bride after eighteen days. Taylor's second (known) wife, Mary Ann Davidson later stated that on the night of their honeymoon, she had caught Taylor trying to remove the newly-purchased wedding-ring from her finger as she slept.

Taylor was subsequently arrested and committed to await trial at the next Assizes, due to be held in Durham in July 1840. At the trial, it emerged that Taylor had defrauded Mary Ann Davidson's father out of several amounts of money, including a £4 loan that Taylor had promised to pay back with interest of £1 per year. The newspaper report of the trial stated that all

An early nineteenth-century woodcut engraving of a marriage proposal. Authors' collection

present were disappointed by the appearance of Taylor, whom many had romantically imagined to be a dashing Lothario. Instead they were treated to the spectacle of a 'shabby-looking individual, with a face not merely ordinary, but repulsive'.

The defendant was completely unabashed and unfazed by his circumstance, even joking with members of the public. He was indicted on two counts: firstly of bigamously marrying Mary Ann Davidson, and secondly of bigamously marrying Mary Ann Wilson. He pleaded 'Not Guilty' to both charges, stating that he was under-age for legal marriage without parental consent, and that therefore none of his three marriages was legal. The defendant conducted his own defence, questioning and arguing with all the prosecution witnesses, including his latest two wives. He was also vociferously supported by his mother, Elizabeth, who had travelled over 100 miles to attend the trial of her son.

The judge and jury were however unimpressed by both Robert and Elizabeth's vocal and impassioned speeches for justice. Taylor was found 'Guilty' and the judge sentenced him to a year's hard labour for the first bigamy, to be followed by another eighteen months' hard labour for the second indictment. 'Lord Kennedy' appeared unconcerned by the sentences, although in fact, due to his youth (he was still under the age of twenty-one) he had been extremely lucky not to receive a far more serious sentence. Indeed, he even had the nerve to ask a parting question of the judge when he was being led out of the courtroom. He was at pains to ask, 'Gentlemen, when I come out, will any of my wives have a claim upon me?'

This was not the end of 'Lord Kennedy's' polygamous career however. On Friday, 18 August 1843 he appeared under his real name at Liverpool Assizes, where he was charged with having bigamously married Deborah Foster of Wigan in the same year. Pre-trial investigation by the Liverpool police had found that Taylor had married yet again in 1842, making a grand total of five marriages within the space of five years, at least four of them bigamous (and it was suggested that this number of marriages did not approach the real total). Taylor's seemingly charmed life and almost infinite good luck ran out at Liverpool however; he was sentenced to seven years' transportation, and seems to have ended his life in Australia. Whether or not he continued his deception overseas upon his release is unfortunately not known. Perhaps he ought to have taken notice of the motto of the real Lord Kennedy, the Earl of Cassilis. The family motto was *Avise la fin* – Consider the end.

The case of 'Lord Kennedy' is entertaining and often humorous. Whilst the plight of the numerous young women that he deceived is to be pitied, one cannot help but think that the avaricious relatives of Taylor's wives got their just deserts, duped by a very cunning and resourceful individual who successfully scammed numerous people for a number of years. That Kennedy could get away with his polygamy for so long seems amazing. Civil registration of marriages was only introduced in 1837 in England; it is interesting to ponder how many more bigamous marriages Taylor could have got away with if the system had not been in place!

CHAPTER 8

The 'Bloody Steps' Murder 1839

On Monday 17 June 1839 the murder of Christina Collins was to lead to the eventual executions, on 11 April 1840, in Stafford Gaol of George Thomas (alias Dobell) aged twenty-seven from Wombourne along with co-accused James Owen. Their executions were witnessed by almost 10,000 people, including almost the whole village of Wombourne. Did two men go to the gallows for a murder that they did not commit? Was the evidence of fact surrounding the death of Christina Collins conclusive? It was certainly the case that the men committed serious sexual assaults on Christina, but were they directly responsible for killing her? This sad tale of how a married woman, on her way to join her husband in London, met with a premature and horrible death seems to have been indicative of a style of life adopted by boatmen, hard drinkers who had little time for religion, and little regard for the law. The chapter title is taken from the set of steps located at the point on the canal where the victim's body was found, and which were used to convey her body to the place her inquest was held.

Christina Collins was a respectable married woman, and her husband was an actor at Covent Garden Theatre. Christina was described by Elizabeth Price, from Liverpool, as a very neat person, a dressmaker by business. Christina joined a canal barge, the *Staffordshire Knot*, at Preston Brook, Cheshire, intending to travel to London, in mid-June 1839. She had been sent money by her husband so that she could join him.

The flyboat on which Mrs Collins travelled was owned by Messrs Pickford & Co, well-known even today in transport circles. The captain of the barge was James Owen, aged thirty-nine, coming from Brinkslow near Rugby. He was well used to canals, having been born on a barge. The other members of the crew were William Ellis (alias Lambert) aged twenty-eight, also from Brinkslow, George Thomas, and William Musson, cabin-boy, aged twelve.

The barge was laden with casks of rum and other goods and began its journey at Preston Brook eventually bound for London. Mrs Collins boarded the barge at dawn, she was described as a woman aged thirty-seven, low in stature, of genteel and respectable appearance and it was apparent that Owen had taken an immediate liking to her. Owen's attraction to Mrs Collins was clearly asserted, so much so that on Sunday at Stoke she complained to William Brooks, one of Pickford's porters, about the 'indecent language and conduct' displayed by the crew and asked about a transfer to a London stage-coach. She stated that she felt herself unsafe while travelling with the crew. Unfortunately there was no place on the stage, so Mrs Collins had little option but to continue the journey on the barge. When the *Staffordshire Knot* reached Stone, on Sunday evening, Mrs Collins again made representations about the behaviour of members of the crew, this time to Mr H Caldwell, the check clerk of the Trent and Mersey Canal Company. His advice was to report the men to Pickfords, but he declined to intervene himself because Owen had such a reputation as a violent man.

This conversation took place the night before the murder, shortly before the barge left Stone. William Musson was soon sent to his bed, and was roused at 5 am on Monday morning by Owen and told to lead the horse, while Owen, Ellis and Thomas negotiated the locks at Colwich, one mile from Rugeley. This was the last time the boy saw Christina Collins alive. Musson stated that the captain afterwards professed to miss the woman from the boat, and that he turned back to 'look for her'. Collins' body was found in the canal at Brindley Bank, about two miles from the Colwich Lock, and one mile from Rugeley, at 5 am on Monday morning.

The statement of Owen was that Mrs Collins repeatedly expressed her determination to commit suicide before she arrived in London, and that he had already thwarted an attempt by pulling her from the canal. Thomas and Ellis in contrast, stated they had not seen her in the water at all. An inquest was held by the coroner, R Fowke, at the *Talbot Inn*, Rugeley, on

The bend at Brindley Bank, around which the Staffordshire Knot *came just before Christina entered the water. The flyboat would have travelled off the picture to the left.* The authors

Tuesday and Wednesday. The medical evidence was that there were no apparent marks of violence on her body, except for slight bruises on each elbow.

There was other evidence given that, at Stoke, she took out a purse 'containing a considerable sum of money, to pay for refreshments'. When she was found she only had 1*s* 6*d*. Musson, fearing for his own life, alerted the Hoo Mill lock-keeper of the tragedy. The lock-keeper, already suspicious, had already reported the incident to the police. It had not taken searchers long to find Collins' body.

The police then turned their attentions to the barge and soon found it abandoned. It is likely that the disappearance of the cabin-boy Musson forced the men to make their getaway and avoid the inevitable. A manhunt was begun in the area, but with no success. Enquiries then focused on the men who had formed the crew, with searches made around the birthplace of each man.

At Smestow Bridge Wombourne, Mrs Thomas, the elderly mother of George, told police she had not seen him for over ten years, since he had run away to join the barge-folk. A thorough search of the cottage was conducted before the police left having found no trace of Thomas. Enquiries into George Thomas revealed that he was the 'black sheep' in an otherwise respectable family. In 1827 the Earl of Dudley had accused him of poaching; this led to a warrant for his arrest, which was still in existence at the time of the murder, and police enquiries to trace Thomas had led to his leaving his mother's cottage.

The first man to be captured was William Ellis, who was found at Brinklow some months later. He denied there had been a murder, declaring that the woman must have fallen overboard. He gave information that Thomas had told him of a 'hidey-hole' at the cottage in Wombourne. A further visit to the cottage was made, this time Thomas was arrested in a small chamber cut into a sandstone cliff at the rear of the cottage. The cottage was located next to the Bridgnorth Road, in front of the cliff. The hidey-hole was accessed by a high screen in the living room and had originally been used as a food-store.

Thomas was weak and very pale following his self-imposed imprisonment and he offered no resistance. He was immedi-

The site of the 'Bloody Steps', these have been replaced on the original site. The authors

ately taken to Stafford Gaol to await trial. Mrs Thomas, his mother died before a charge of wilfully harbouring a fugitive could be laid. The last man to be captured was James Owen. He made the mistake of visiting his parents and wife, who lived together at Brinklow and was arrested. All three men were now in custody at Stafford.

There was now a wait until the trial of the men, which took place at the beginning of April 1840. Mr Serjeant Ludlow and Mr Lee appeared for the prosecution, with Mr Godson and Mr Yardley for the defence. The Judge was Baron Gurney. Mr Ludlow stated that there were only three ways of accounting for the death – accident, suicide or the wilful death at the hands of one or more of the men. Early evidence was given by William Brooks and Hugh Caldwell. Then the court heard from Thomas Brewer, captain of a boat called *Emma*. He had met Owens boat and Thomas got onto *Emma* for a glass of ale. Brewer spoke to the woman and Thomas is alleged to have said 'Jemmy (Owen) had had concerns with her, and he would that night, or they'd Burke her' (kill her and not leave any marks on her, so-named after the activities of William Burke, the Edinburgh murderer and body-snatcher).

Ann Mills, Hoo Mill lock-keeper, heard a cry at midnight. She saw a woman on the top of a boat in the lock, belonging to Pickfords, there were three men with it and the woman got off the boat. She cried for her shoes, and once she got them she sat outside the cabin with her legs hanging down, she said to the men 'Don't attempt me; I'll not go into the cabin'. One of the men was asked who she was; the reply was that she was a passenger with her husband. James Mills, husband of Ann, gave evidence to corroborate his wife.

When a boat captain called James Wilday was cross-examined by Mr Godson, he was asked about the possibility that someone not used to boat travel might have been thrown off, if the horse jerked, at the sharp turn at Brindley Bank. The reply was given that it was difficult to keep one's standing on the bend. Christina Collins body was found about eighty yards beyond Brindley Bank. Two boatmen, Thomas Grant and John Johnson, found the body in the water, lying face down. The canal was about thirty-four-feet-wide and the water about three-feet-ten-inches-deep at its deepest at the point where she was found.

Mr Barnett, surgeon of Rugeley, examined the body and he noted small bruises on the right arm and water in her stomach. In his opinion she was alive when she went into the water and that death was suffocation by drowning. He said this was not decisive but 'generally as he stated'.

William Musson also gave evidence. He stated that he got out at Colwich Lock to go to the horse; Christina was in the cabin at this point, with her shoes and bonnet off. When they reached Brindley Bank the woman was not there, Owen was steering and they navigated the turn as usual. When he asked where the woman was Owen told him he believed she was drowned. In cross-examination Musson said when the boat reached Brindley Bank Ellis was asleep, snoring.

Charles Robotham, a Pickford clerk at Fradley, further down the canal, said that about 6 am on Monday morning Owen told him a woman had drowned herself, and had attempted it once before. Owen was unwilling to go back and look for her. Robotham went on to Fazeley, arriving before the boat. At Fazeley the police became involved and a constable searched the boat. Christina's bonnet and shoes were found in the cabin.

Christina's husband, Robert, gave evidence that he had sent his wife a sovereign for her to come to London; he also formally identified her body. Another witness to give evidence was Joseph Orgill, convicted and pardoned for bigamy. Orgill was in prison with Owen, and Owen allegedly told him that Ellis and Thomas had raped and mauled Collins to death. Owen also said that Collins was dead on the boat; he was not clear about whether she rolled off the boat or was pushed.

In summing up for the defence, Mr Godson said he believed the men were being tried twice for murder. Firstly, they were being tried for drowning her. Secondly, the prosecution were alleging that she was killed whilst she was still on the boat. His question for the jury was whether it had been proved that all three had drowned her or any of them before she went into the water. He urged the jury to give the men the benefit of the doubt. The judge reminded the jury that their first object was not conviction of the guilty, put protection of the innocent. The

The view south away from Brindley Bank, possibly the nearest spot to where the body was found.
The authors

jury retired to consider their verdict. They returned in only half-an-hour, and found all three guilty of murder. The men were all condemned to death. The judge told the men to 'look not for pardon in this world'.

On the morning that he was due to be executed a respite came for Ellis, the reason for which is not known. He was only told of this when the three were taken to the prison chapel to partake of the Sacrament. On hearing the news Ellis shook his two co-prisoners by the hand; Owen wept uncontrollably, but Thomas gave Ellis advice in a firm voice, saying 'Bill, thee'st got off – but let this be a warning to thee as long as thee livest'.

Thomas and Owen then went to the gallows, and it is said that nearly 10,000 people gathered to witness the executions. Both men were buried within the walls of the gaol, as was customary with executed prisoners, who could not be buried in consecrated ground. The executioner on this occasion was William Calcraft, who negotiated with the governor of Stafford Gaol to use a prisoner, George Smith, as his assistant. The man who was due to assist Calcraft had failed to turn up to perform his duty, owing to him being too drunk to assist.

George Smith, who became the 'Dudley Hangman', originally came from Rowley Regis in the Black Country; he was in prison at Stafford as he was in debt. He went on to become an executioner himself, learning his trade from Calcraft. His most famous 'victim' was 'Palmer the Poisoner' of Rugeley, who was hanged at Stafford in 1856.

There was a report that Christina Collins' body was found with a heavy length of chain wrapped around her. This chain was said to have been made for Pickfords by Joseph Barnsley at Cradley Heath, and was later proved to have been issued to 'the *Staffordshire Knot*'. Markings on the chain proved the issue, a measure implemented to reduce the widespread theft of such items. This fact does not appear in the accounts I have read of the trial.

Christina's grave, in St Augustine's church in Rugeley, has a headstone which bears the following inscription:

To the memory of Christina Collins wife of Robert Collins, London. Who having been most barbarously treated was found dead in the canal in this Parish on 17 June 1839 Aged thirty-seven years. This stone is erected by some individuals of the Parish of Rugeley in commemoration of the end of this unhappy woman.

The churchyard also contains the family vault of William Palmer, whose remains were buried in the grounds of Stafford Gaol. At least two of Palmer's victims are buried at St Augustine's – Leonard Bladen and John Parsons Cook, who was a friend of Palmer.

The bend in the canal where Christina's body was found has a marker indicating the fact. It is a ninety-degree bend, which lends credence to the possibility that she fell off the barge. The 'Bloody Steps' are a few yards away from the bend. Both the

The grave of Christina Collins, to be found in St Augustine's churchyard, Rugeley.
The authors

prosecution and defence evidence is somewhat contradictory. The prosecution allege Christina was alive when she was thrown into the water, this would tend to be supported by the medical evidence of water in the lungs. However, given the depth (or lack) of water, it seems likely that there would be more noticeable injuries to the body. On the other hand, if Christina was dead when she entered the water, how does this account for water in her lungs? Also, how did she die, again given the relatively minor injuries noted by the doctor?

The other mystery is why Ellis was given a reprieve on the day of his execution. What is certain is that Mr Passmore, Solicitor for the defendants, wrote to the Home Secretary, Lord Normanby, asking for a reprieve for each of the men. He pointed out the 'doubtful nature of the evidence', going on to state there was no evidence that they had actually drowned Christina, or had otherwise occasioned her death. The judge declared the case was one he would not be justified in interfering to prevent the law from taking its course.

Mr Passman won a temporary reprieve for each of the men, for one week, to allow him to place further information before Lord Normanby. He raised the point that the jury relied on the evidence of the surgeon, who had admitted his decision was not decisive. A week later Mr Passman received a further communication from Lord Normanby, indicating that there were no grounds to justify him recommending the prisoners to the mercy of the Crown.

A number of barristers also visited the gaol. They expressed extreme doubt about the case against Ellis, and explored means to prevent his execution. Mr Gaunt was despatched for a final interview with Lord Normanby. All three prisoners declared Ellis was innocent; although Ellis did admit attempting to rape Christina. Musson had also given evidence that he heard Ellis snoring at around the time she would have 'fallen' from the boat; Ellis himself stated he was asleep at the time of her death. This appeal must have worked, as on the morning of the execution his respite arrived, just before the executions were scheduled.

One of the most famous fictional detectives of our time has also investigated this case. Inspector Morse in Colin Dexter's

The Wench is Dead carried out an investigation. The names and location of the incident were changed, but the facts were largely taken from a pamphlet written after the trial by one of the defence barristers. Morse found evidence to clear the men, and further evidence that implicated her husband.

CHAPTER 9

'Damn Her; if Her won't go, Chain Her to the Post!' The Strange Case of Eliza Price and the two Petty Sessions 1845

This chapter illustrates an unusual case; one in which the forces of law and order are called to account, and one in which a member of the working class managed to get her grievance heard before the House of Commons, resulting in a Parliamentary Inquiry. The case is also of interest in that it highlights the problems of maintaining what was a parish-based judicial and law-enforcement system in a rapidly industrialising and increasingly populous area. We are allowed glimpses of a time when the powers-that-be were gradually realising that systems which had remained fundamentally unchanged since their foundations in mediaeval times were unsuitable for a country undergoing the throes of the Industrial Revolution.

On Friday 9 May 1845 Mr T Duncombe MP (a well-known campaigning politician, nicknamed 'Honest Tom', who had been given the distinction of introducing the Chartists' Petition to the House of Commons in 1842) read out another petition that was to have far-reaching consequences. The petition had been submitted on behalf of Mrs Eliza Price of Brierley Hill, and contained allegations of police brutality and judicial ineptitude against Mrs Price, who at the time of the incident was seven months pregnant.

The petition caused uproar in the House, with one Member of Parliament stating that 'a case of greater oppression than that stated in the petition had never occurred. It was a disgrace to the magistrates and the laws of the country'. An official investigation by Commissioner F. Newman Rogers was hurriedly instigated and his findings were subsequently published as a Select Committee Report.

The investigation took place on 30 and 31 May 1845 and was held at the *Cross Inn*, Kingswinford in closed session. Those present included Mr and Mrs Price, two police constables, Mr Samuel Stone Briscoe (local worthy and magistrate at Kingswinford Petty Sessions) and his 'professional adviser'. Those present heard the following evidence:

> *On Thursday 3 April 1845, Eliza, the wife of William Price, attended at the Petty Sessions, held at the Cross Inn, Kingswinford, as a witness on behalf of a female neighbour (Mrs Beaumont), who was charged with having assaulted and threatened Joseph Newey, a common informer. Whilst passing through the crowd in the justice room, Newey put his hand on Mrs Price's shoulder and turned her round in order to make way for himself – conduct which Mrs Price resented, pushing or striking him in the side, whereupon Newey immediately pushed her violently on the bosom; Mr Briscoe, the sitting magistrate, who partially saw what was going forward, called to Newey by name, and checked him in a tone of rebuke [. . .]. Mrs Price, much irritated and rather loudly, was taken out of the room by a policeman, becoming faint and unwell, she being six or seven months advanced in pregnancy.*

After recovering, Mrs Price applied for a summons against Newey for assault, but Mr Briscoe, who was of the opinion that Mrs Price had been the aggressor, refused to issue one. Mrs Price, understandably somewhat disgruntled, then walked home with her husband. After sleeping on it she was not content to let the matter rest, and on the following day she obtained a summons for the affair from other magistrates who were in session at nearby Wordsley, less than two miles from Mr Briscoe's court. On 7 April the summons was heard at Wordsley Petty Sessions before William Robins, William Foster and George Bate, with Joseph Newey being fined and bound over to keep the peace (William Robins was a nephew of Mr Benjamin Robins of Dunsley, who was the victim in the Gibbet Lane murder of 1812).

The Cross, *Kingswinford, site of Kingswinford Petty Sessions in 1845.* The authors

However, Mr Newey had on the same day already obtained a warrant from Mr Briscoe against Mrs Price for abusive behaviour. Eliza Price's petition states 'that after the said conviction of the said Joseph Newey (at Wordsley), he, the said Joseph Newey, exultingly pulled a paper from his pocket'. Mr Newey must have congratulated himself on his quick-wittedness in scoring a victory over Mrs Price.

As a result of this warrant, Constables James Baker and William Onions of the recently formed Staffordshire County Constabulary (established in October 1842) called on Eliza at her house at around 6 pm. Constables Baker and Onions obviously took their jobs very seriously, both perhaps being anxious to make a good impression with their superiors in the newly created force. Eliza was informed that she would have to accompany the constables into custody. Her husband, together with a parish constable, Mr Tomkinson, were present and both men asked the police officers to release Eliza on assurances of her keeping her appointment with the Kingswinford magis-trates, but the officers refused. They insisted that Mrs Price accompany them to the *Horseshoes Inn* in High Street, Brierley Hill, where it was planned that Mrs Price would be kept under 'house arrest' until her hearing at the Kingswinford Petty Sessions, which were due to be held the following morning. Mr Price and Mr Tomkinson insisted on accompanying the police constables as they took Mrs Price from her house.

On arrival at the inn, the party found that unfortunately no room was available, and Constable Baker suggested that Eliza accompany him to his house, where she could sleep in a room with his wife. Eliza understandably refused this offer, as it was by this time after midnight and she did not want to travel with an unknown man at that time of night to a strange house. Constable Onions, obviously put out by the unforeseen difficulties of dealing with Mrs Price was then alleged by her to have said to his colleague, Constable Baker, 'Damn her; if her won't go, chain her to the post!'. Constable Baker then went out and returned with a pair of handcuffs and a length of iron dog-chain:

> One handcuff was bolted around Eliza's wrist which was furthest from the fire, and the chain attached to it, passing across her body, was fastened to an iron post which supported the fireplace.

The heavily pregnant Eliza Price remained in this uncomfortable situation until 7 or 8 am: accounts differing as to whether or not she was supplied with bedding and a place to lie down. Eliza's petition states that:

> no bed, bed-clothes, or other accommodation for sleeping was provided your petitioner, except a wooden bench, which was of an inconvenient distance from the post, and was immovable.

She was then taken on foot over four miles to Mr Briscoe's house, Fir Tree House, where she was released without bail. She subsequently appeared before Mr Briscoe and two other magistrates at Kingswinford Petty Sessions on 17 April, when she was discharged. This ended Mrs Price's unnecessary and harrowing ordeal, but she was obviously made of stern stuff, and determined not to let the matter rest. She must have sought legal advice (from whom it is unfortunately not clear – at the time it was very unusual for a member of the working class to

High Street, Brierley Hill, c.1920. The building that was the Horseshoes Inn
can be seen on the extreme right of the photograph. Authors' collection

gain access to such professional opinion) and it was decided
that her best course of action would be to petition the House
of Commons in order to bring her grievances to the widest
possible audience.

The petition was reported in *The Times* of 11 May 1845, and
a letter from Mr Briscoe in which he defended his actions
swiftly appeared on 13 May, stating that:

> *The result of the enquiry, I feel confident, will show that I have
> not acted illegally or harshly in any degree whatever. Trusting to
> your sense of justice for the insertion of this note.*

In his defence given to the subsequent official inquiry that
resulted from the petition, Mr Briscoe stated that 'it is the usual
practice to issue warrants and not summonses in all cases of
assault'. He admitted that he did not know that the case had
been dealt with and disposed of by the magistrates at Wordsley,

or of Mrs Price's incarceration, saying that she had not mentioned it to him.

Constable Baker stated bluntly that he had no option but to chain Eliza up, as she had refused to promise to appear before Mr Briscoe, and that Mrs Ann Pearsall, the landlady of the *Horseshoes Inn* 'would not allow her to be left in the house except she was chained up'. Interestingly, Mrs Pearsall's husband William must have found this episode fascinating, as he later became one of the first Brierley Hill constables employed in the Staffordshire Constabulary.

Constable Onions for his part denied the 'coarse expressions imputed to him, but he admitted that he had 'advised Baker to chain her up, as he had been in the habit of doing for years, there being no lock-up house in the neighbourhood, or other means of securing prisoners'. This statement concerning the lack of suitably secure accommodation is backed up by a report relating to a slightly earlier period. Thomas Clulow, a well-known local historian, remarked in his *Journal* that in the 1830s the *Old Bush Inn* in Level Street, Brierley Hill had also often been used as a lock-up by the then parish constable, Benjamin Greenfield:

> *Mr Greenfield's house was the 'lock-up', with a chain fastened to the culprit's leg, and locked to the fire grate, all night. On the next morning, he would be removed to Stourbridge lock-up, or taken to Kingswinford, to appear before Mr Briscoe, magistrate.*

Commissioner Newman Rogers stated that Mr Briscoe should be exonerated of any deliberate ill-will toward Mrs Price, but severely criticised him for not 'rebuking the constables for such unnecessary rigour in the execution of a warrant on so trivial a charge'. Constable Baker was found to have 'acted from a mistaken sense of duty ... for from the beginning to the end his manner was described by Mrs Price to have been civil and forbearing'. For his part, Constable Onions was found innocent of all ill-will – the Commissioner further remarked that (as Constable Onions had claimed):

> *Indeed, the system of chaining prisoners seems to be familiar to the people of the district, for neither Eliza Price nor her husband appears to have considered that she had undergone any peculiar*

injury in this respect. Their grievance was that she was brought up before the magistrates at the Cross Inn on 17 April for the same assault which had been determined in her favour by the magistrates at Wordsley on 7 April.

Commissioner Newman Rogers' detailed report also investigated other areas of misconduct by the local magistracy, highlighting many shortcomings and anomalies of the judicial system. The inquiry had highlighted a very unusual situation in which two apparently competing Petty Sessions were operating within a radius of a few miles. He detailed a rift that had occurred between several local magistrates due to a breakdown of communication:

Previously to the year 1834, the business of the Kingswinford district was done at Wolverhampton or Dudley, or, when the nature of the business admitted, at Stourbridge, which is in Worcestershire, by the Worcestershire magistrates, who were also magistrates of Staffordshire. In August 1834 Petty Sessions were established at the Cross Inn by Mr Briscoe and Mr Cope, magistrates living in the immediate neighbourhood [this rift resulted from an argument with the Stourbridge magistrates over clerks' fees].

In January 1844, Petty Sessions were established on each Monday by the Stourbridge magistrates in Wordsley at a former Dissenting Chapel:

and resolutions to that effect were entered into, which resolutions being published and circulated in hand-bills, a counter hand-bill was circulated, dated 11 February 1844, stating that the Petty Sessions would continue to be heard at the Cross Inn on Thursdays, signed by Mr Briscoe and three other magistrates.

Samuel Stone Briscoe and the other three magistrates were clearly not happy at having their authority in the district challenged.

The Commissioner pointed out the obvious shortcomings of having two conflicting Petty Sessions within the same district:

Two Petty Sessions being thus established under the circumstances above stated, without any division of district, unseeming jealousies among the magistrates and conflicts of authority as must naturally have been expected, have frequently occurred, tending to bring into disrepute the administration of justice.

He therefore recommended that a division of 'the populous district which is now the subject of contention between two conflicting Benches of Magistrates' was urgently needed. He was highly critical of the conduct of Mr Briscoe, who conducted magisterial business from his own home, rather than from an official site of justice, and who also appeared to have issued warrants without filling in the details of the crime of which the recipient was accused – this was indeed an extremely serious omission that could have led to widespread abuse of the judicial system.

The newly created Staffordshire County Constabulary also received criticism for its handling of the affair. As a result of this criticism, Colonel Gilbert Hogg, chairman of the Kingswinford district police force and Deputy Constable of the County Constabulary caused the following addition to be entered into the order book of the Kingswinford Police Station on 25 July 1845:

No prisoner should in future be chained to the grate, but that one police constable should remain on reserve duty to take charge of the prisoner, and that all prisoners shall, as soon as possible, be removed to the Kingswinford lock-up.

However, this probably did not completely remove the abhorrent practice, as there were apparently still parish constables (employed by the local parish rather than the County) who continued to chain people; Commissioner Newman Rogers wrote that 'other constables (of whom there seems to be still a considerable proportion) adhere to the former practice'.

Colonel Hogg also complained that whilst Kingswinford district contained over 22,000 inhabitants, the single lock-up available could only hold six people. Colonel Hogg's reputation itself does not appear to have been tarnished by this incident; he became Chief Officer of Wolverhampton Borough Police Force from 1848–1857, and then became Chief Constable of Staffordshire until 1866.

The recommendations of Commissioner Newman Rogers were passed on to Sir James Graham, Secretary of State for the Home Office. He in turn wrote a letter dated 30 June 1845 to Earl Talbot, Lord Lieutenant of Staffordshire, requesting him to ensure that the recommendations were implemented in full and that the local magistracy and constabulary were made aware of their shortcomings. No mention is made in the records of any compensation or apology to Eliza Price.

CHAPTER 10

'Jem, I Hope You will Die as well as Me': The Slaying of Catherine Morris 1851

This case is a classic one of a lover spurned and a fallen woman. The events and circumstances illustrate the extreme lengths to which people can be driven for love. Unlike several of the previous cases, there is no mystery in this one; it is simply a story of two people who, in different circumstances, may have lived a happy life together.

On Monday 9 June 1851, a tragic tale unfolded in Wolverhampton. Catherine Morris, a woman who had fallen on hard times and who was described as being of 'the lowest class of prostitute', was sitting in the *Brown Bear* public house in Lichfield Street. She was flanked by two men; a Mr Lawson and a man known simply as 'Steve'. Although she had been brought a few drinks, she was a persistent alcoholic and had not yet reached the stage of incoherence.

Earlier in the day, Catherine and a man called James Sones, who lodged with her in a brothel-cum-lodging-house in nearby Berry Street, had been seen vehemently arguing in the street. Their language had been so strong that passers-by had intervened to stop them continuing. The quarrel seems to have arisen over Catherine Morris's determination to continue her career of prostitution despite the fact that she had formed a romantic attachment with James, and appeared to have lived with him as man and wife for a period.

Their relationship had been soured by the fact that Catherine, whilst in an alcoholic stupor, had some time ago allowed a young child of hers to be burnt to death through her drunken negligence. James, although not the father of the child,

Lichfield Street, Wolverhampton, c.1870 (Note the gentleman looking at the shop window, who appears with his 'ghost' due to the slow exposure of the photograph). Reproduced with permission from the collections of Wolverhampton Archives & Local Studies

had treated it as though it were his own and was understandably upset about its death.

The arguing couple met again on the evening of 9 June in the *Brown Bear* at around 7.30 pm. James became increasingly agitated at the sight of his loved one being courted by two men and approached Catherine, demanding his property back. Catherine insultingly removed a handkerchief from her person and threw it down on the table in front of her. James angrily replied that he didn't mean simply his handkerchief; he wanted to collect all his possessions from their lodgings, implying that he was finally leaving her.

At this, Catherine rose from her seat and the two estranged lovers left the public house by the rear entrance and entered an alley-way that led from the back of the *Brown Bear* to Berry Street. One of the men to whom Catherine had been chatting, Mr Lawson, decided to follow them as he could see that they were both extremely upset (although neither was drunk). Some-way down the alley in front of him, Lawson saw James put his right hand around Catherine's neck and reach his hand up to her forehead, pulling her head back as though to kiss her.

However, this was not James' intention. Instead, he suddenly brought his left hand across Catherine's throat in a sweeping motion and she dropped to the ground.

Lawson rushed to her aid, to find her throat slashed with a gaping wound some seven inches long and an inch deep. Catherine managed to call out to him 'Stop that man, he has murdered me!' James made no attempt to escape or discard the clasp knife that he held in his left hand.

Catherine was carried to another nearby public house, the *Black Horse* in Berry Street, where a surgeon, James Gatis, managed to stop the bleeding from the wound in her throat. James Sones accompanied her to the *Black Horse*, where he begged to see Catherine. As he approached her, expressing his sorrow at his actions, she weakly said 'Jem, I hope you will die as well as me'. The constabulary was called and Sones offered no resistance to his arrest and incarceration at Wolverhampton Gaol. He was subsequently moved to Stafford Gaol on Wednesday, 11 June, where he was committed for trial for attempted murder. This charge was subsequently altered to one

Stafford Gaol. Some of the original buildings of the nineteenth-century gaol (including the gatehouse) can just be seen behind the twentieth-century high walls. The authors

of 'wilful murder' after Catherine, who had been taken to hospital, died of her injuries on Thursday morning.

James Sones, who was twenty-six years old, was brought down from Stafford to be formally charged at Wolverhampton by Colonel Gilbert Hogg of the Wolverhampton constabulary (this was the same Colonel Hogg who gave evidence to the parliamentary inquiry into the treatment of Eliza Price in 1845). Colonel Hogg stated at Sones' trial that the defendant constantly asked to see the body of Catherine before she was buried; he asked at least twenty times, and Hogg finally relented. Sones broke down when he saw the body of his lover and expressed considerable remorse for his actions.

His trial took place at Stafford on 30 July 1851. Sones was described as a navvy, although his defence was paid for by Mr Robert Ransome of Ransome's, a large firm based in Ipswich that manufactured agricultural implements. Ransome's was founded by Robert Ransome's father, also named Robert, in 1789, who was a Quaker and who operated a paternalistic system of employment similar to that of the Cadbury family in Birmingham. The firm was the first in Britain to manufacture lawnmowers and continued in family ownership until 1998.

It appears that Sones had previously been employed by Ransome's and that the firm's paternalism extended to paying for his defence counsel. Sones is a surname that originated in Suffolk, so it seems likely that James Sones had been employed by the firm in Ipswich before moving to the Black Country.

Sones was described in the *Staffordshire Advertiser* as being 'tall and good-looking – nothing in his countenance to indicate the murderer'. This sentence reflects a belief prevalent at the time that ones physiognomy reflected one's inner self, whether base or noble. After the publication of Darwin's *On The Origin of Species* in 1859, scientific thought was increasingly devoted to the study of the human animal; 'sciences' such as phrenology and physiognomy enjoyed something of a resurgence after their original flourishes in the late eighteenth century. This in turn led to several scientists promulgating the idea that not only was there a distinct 'criminal class', but that this class could be recognised by attributes such as facial features and lack of intellect – Henry Maudsley's treatise entitled *Responsibility in Mental Disease* of 1874 went so far as to state that 'individuals are born with such a flaw of warp of nature that all the care in the world will not prevent them from being vicious or criminal'. There was therefore a move from attempts to create social reform in order to dissuade the perceived criminal element from becoming recidivists to a media-generated bugbear of a race of biologically determined criminal savages, intent upon wrecking the very fabric of society. This fear has never quite left society's psyche – one only has to look at the banner headlines in today's more lurid tabloid publications to sense that this fear of the unknown or the different (especially if foreign and different) is still very much with us.

Sones pleaded not guilty to 'Wilful Murder' though he did not deny that he had killed Catherine. His defence was very ably handled, and the judge and jury decided that the indictment should be reduced to that of manslaughter. Considerable sympathy for him was evinced within the court, and it was made clear that his was not a premeditated attack, but rather an unfortunate snap decision that had appalling consequences for all concerned. The circumstances of Catherine Morris' life undoubtedly contributed to the view of the judge and jury. Quite apart from the plethora of discriminatory legal differences between the sexes the State undoubtedly maintained double standards in its dealing with men and women.

From at least the eighteenth century onward there was, as Frank McLynn has stated in his book *Crime and Punishment in Eighteenth-Century England,* an 'assumption that the entire weight of social censure for 'illicit' sexuality should descend upon them [women].' Further evidence of this inequality is implicit in the often almost insurmountable difficulties that faced women when they wished to prosecute for rape or other sexual offences during the nineteenth and much of the twentieth centuries. Catherine Morris's chosen profession of prostitution would have certainly lessened sympathy for her fate; a woman's fall from the pedestal of wholesome maternity and probity to the gutter of prostitution and petty theft was almost universally adjudged to be greater than that of a man's.

However, Sones was not allowed to escape without punishment for his actions and he was subsequently found 'Guilty' of manslaughter and sentenced to transportation to Australia for life.

As a transportee, Sones was one of almost 163,000 men, women and children who were sentenced to be sent abroad. Transportation from the shores of Britain had started in the mid-eighteenth century, and early transportees were sent to Britain's American colonies. However, following the loss of the colony after the disastrous War of Independence, transportation moved to Australia and on 13 May 1787 the 'First Fleet' of transportation ships set sail on the 16,000 mile journey that was to take eight months.

Many Australians are today proud to state that their ancestors came to Australia as transportees and to be able to claim that one's ancestor was a part of the first such contingent, a 'First Fleeter', holds a certain cachet, similar to that of

Memorial plaque commemorating the transportation of Sarah Bellamy of Belbroughton as part of the first fleet to convey convicts to Australia. The authors

Americans who are descended from the first settlers who travelled on the *Mayflower*. A popular saying is that 'Australians had their ancestors chosen for them by some of the best judges in the country'! However, at the time it must have been a truly frightening and horrendous journey, during which many convicts perished.

Of the 759 convicts on the voyage, one came from the outskirts of the Black Country. Sarah Bellamy aged fifteen of Belbroughton was tried at Worcester on 9 July 1785 for stealing a purse containing cash and promissory notes. She was sentenced to seven years' transportation and became a 'First Fleeter' on the ship *Lady Penrhyn*. She married a fellow convict, James Bloodman in 1790 and eventually had seven children, although four died in infancy. At the time of her death in 1843, she and her husband were regarded as most respectable inhabitants of Australia.

James Sones shared his sentence of transportation with several other Black Country individuals in July 1851. Mary Detheridge, aged nineteen, was found guilty of stealing a shawl in Rowley Regis and sentenced to seven years' transportation (it is not known if Mary was any relation of the Rowley Regis constable James Detheridge, who arrested Susannah Perry for the murder of her husband in 1838). Similarly, George Robinson stole two pairs of boots in Tipton and was also sentenced to seven years' transportation. In total, many hundreds of Black Country folk were transported to Australia, leaving in their wake numerous destitute and devastated families, who were destined never to see their loved ones again.

The system of transportation (which also involved sending convicts to other areas of the world, such as parts of Africa) was finally ended in 1868, when the equally reprehensible system of public hanging was also abolished.

It is not known what happened to James Sones after his sentence. Although he committed an awful crime, leading to the death of his lover, it is possible to feel a degree of sympathy for both James and Catherine. Perhaps if their circumstances had been more favourable, both of their lives would have been happier.

CHAPTER 11

A Dudley Murder
1855

The Earl of Dudley said in 1855 'the foulest crime it has been my misfortune to discover and designing of the driest form of retribution the law can exact'. He was talking about the murder of a Woodside girl of seventeen, Mary Ann Mason, by her boyfriend, twenty-three-year-old Joe Meadows in the notorious Sailor's Return Inn *in Cromwell Street, Kate's Hill, Dudley. Jealousy was the motive for her murder, and the full weight of justice was quickly exacted on her killer. What is obvious is that the incident resulted in the unnecessary waste of two young lives.*

Mary was a dark-haired beauty from Woodside, a mining hamlet halfway between Dudley and Brierley Hill. Her father was a lay preacher and was not pleased when Mary began working as a kitchen-maid at the *Sailor's Return*. The owner, a former Dudley prize-fighter and engine-smith, William Hunt and his wife Mary, had taken Mary Mason on as a servant seven weeks prior, and Mary was living at the *Sailor's Return* as a member of the family.

Hunt paid Mary her wages on the explicit understanding that the young woman, who was quite a beauty, would not become romantically attached to any of the young men who courted her in the *Sailor's Return*. He possibly saw marriage bringing an end to his profitable run, as Mary was apparently a source of interest for customers to the inn. This arrangement was to prove financially lucrative for Hunt.

Joseph Meadows worked as a whitesmith for Joseph Rann, a small Dudley galvaniser and member of the local yeomanry, from the Round Oak area of Woodside. Meadows also took board and lodgings with Rann. Meadows quickly became besotted with Mary, and began escorting her home to Woodside, she apparently returning his affection. Meadows soon became more serious and at the time of the murder Mary had been 'receiving the addresses' of Meadows for about ten months.

In order to get round the obstacle of the agreement with Hunt, Meadows was introduced as the brother of Mary, and Hunt and his wife were taken in by this ruse. He became a regular visitor at the tavern, but soon began to regret the declared relationship with Mary. They would argue bitterly when he saw the way she behaved with men who were customers at the inn. Mary played strongly on this jealousy that Meadows felt and she began to play to her audience. Some of her admirers began to buy drinks for Joseph; this was an obvious ploy to get into his 'sister's' good books. This smouldering situation was inflamed because Mary treated Joseph as a nuisance of a brother, someone who cramped her style when she was with her favourite customers. The scene was set for the situation to reach a volatile conclusion.

The relationship became rocky; Mary wanted to end it, Joseph began to drink heavily and his work was neglected. It would only be a matter of time before the situation reached a head. On the evening of Saturday, 12 May 1855 Meadows had been present in the *Sailor's Return*, Mary was avoiding his gaze. William Hunt said later that when Meadows entered, Mary hid behind him as though she did not want to see him. Meadows left the inn in the early hours of Sunday, 13 May; he went home to Round Oak. Joseph Rann said that Meadows arrived at about 2 am, intoxicated, and did not go to bed, staying downstairs on the sofa.

Sometime between 6 and 7 am on Sunday 13 May Meadows returned to the *Sailor's Return*. William Hunt heard him arrive and served him with a pint of ale. Meadows went into the kitchen where Mary was already at work mopping the floor; he sat down with his drink but, did not say anything. A short while later sometime just after 8 am, two miners, William Ingram and William Robinson, entered the kitchen of the inn, having just finished work. They sat drinking not five feet away from Meadows, and noticed that there was no conversation between Joseph and Mary. At about 9 am Ingram stated he heard a gunshot from inside the kitchen and saw Mary fall to the floor. He turned toward the sound of the shot and saw Meadows

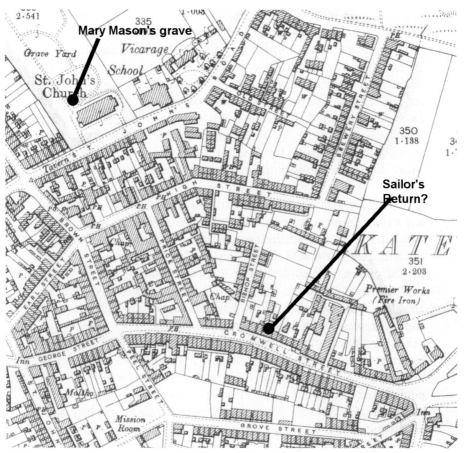

Part of Kate's Hill from the 1901 OS map. Back in 1855 hardly any of the houses between the church and the Sailor's Return were built. An 1853 plan shows the church and a new street, which I believe is Cromwell Street. Authors' collection

lowering a 'piece' (a carbine) to the ground. Ingram said to Meadows 'Oh, you rogue, what have you done, you have shot that wench'. Meadows replied 'I have another revolver in my pocket' and made no attempt to escape. Robinson was despatched quickly to fetch the police and medical assistance was also called for. Hunt and his wife quickly entered the kitchen, having also heard the shot.

Mr Richard Meredith, doctor and assistant to Mr Cochrane, arrived soon after and began to try and treat Mary's wounds. Superintendent Jewkes from the Dudley Constabulary (probably the same Jewkes who as a constable had attended the death of Samuel Perry in 1838) also arrived within a few minutes and took Meadows into custody, quickly charging him with the crime of murder. Meadows replied 'I have had my revenge, which they tell me is sweet, and I am satisfied'. On the way to the police station Meadows indicated that jealousy was his motive, saying 'if I did not have her nobody else should'. He also disclosed that he had been in possession of a revolver whilst in the *Sailor's Return* the previous evening, intending to kill Mary and then shoot himself, but the opportunity did not present itself.

A few days after the horrific murder Meadows appeared before magistrates for committal proceedings. The magistrates heard the evidence of the two miners, Ingram and Robinson. William Robinson said that after Meadows had placed the gun on the ground, he took charge of it and handed it to William Hunt. Meadows said to Robinson 'she should have given me an answer'. A revolver was found in Meadows' pocket when he was later searched whilst still in the kitchen.

Richard Meredith also gave evidence, stating that there was a large wound under Mary's left eye, bleeding profusely, there were other gunshot wounds to the face, and he removed several pieces of shot while she was still alive. Mary did not speak and within fifteen minutes of being shot she was dead. Mr Johnson, assisted by Meredith, carried out the post-mortem. They had no doubt that death was by gunshot. Some of the shot had entered the auditory canal and had broken the temple into fragments. The carotidal artery had also been ruptured close to where it entered the skull; the jugular vein was also severed.

Joseph Rann gave evidence at the hearing that he noticed Meadows had left his house before 7 am on the Sunday morning. Rann also confirmed that the carbine belonged to him. He possessed the weapon to use as part of his yeomanry duties.

When all the evidence had been heard Mr Fereday, one of the magistrates, said to Meadows 'you stand committed to take your trial at the next assizes for the County of Worcester for the wilful murder of Mary Ann Mason'. Later the same day Coroner W Robinson held an inquest on the body of Mary Ann

Mason, at the *Sailor's Return*. The same evidence that committed Meadows to the Assizes was heard by the jury, who returned a verdict of 'wilful murder'. Meadows was then committed on the Coroner's warrant to Worcester Assizes.

Two days after she was murdered Mary Ann Mason was laid to rest at St John's Church, Kate's Hill, not far from the place of her death. Her funeral was attended by a large crowd of local people and a headstone was later erected by voluntary subscriptions:

> *To the memory of Mary Ann Mason who was murdered by Joseph Meadows on 12 May 1855 aged seventeen years*

On Tuesday 17 July 1855 the trial of Joseph Meadows took place before Chief Baron Pollock at Worcester. Mr Widdlestone and Mr Cresswell appeared for the Crown, while Mr Kettle defended Meadows.

The grave of Mary Ann Mason; it is in poor condition and the inscription difficult to read. The churchyard itself is overgrown and largely neglected. The authors

Joseph Rann identified the carbine as his, and stated that he had checked his home and found that two flasks of powder and shot, together with some percussion caps were missing, along with the carbine. William Ingram identified the carbine as the weapon Meadows had fired in the kitchen. Superintendent Jewkes said he found a powder flask and some percussion caps when he searched Meadows. On the way to the police station Meadows told Superintendent Jewkes 'I pulled the carbine from behind my back, and fired it off in an instant. I threw it down to pick the girl up, but was prevented'.

William Hunt also gave evidence, that on hearing the gunshot he ran into the kitchen and collared Meadows. He said 'Oh, you vagabond, you have shot your own sister'. Meadows replied 'I've done what I intended to do'. Mr Kettle had a very difficult task in defending his client. He urged the jury not to convict Meadows of murder as he had been intoxicated when he had made his admissions. The Judge summed up the case in great detail. The jury were sent out to deliberate, and took just five minutes before they returned with a 'guilty' verdict to the charge of 'wilful murder'.

Whilst awaiting execution Meadows wrote to Mary's parents:

I know I have committed the most dreadful deed that man can be guilty of against God and you all, and especially against one that was a most kind and affectionate sister to all of you. I believe it has caused many an aching heart, but I hope and trust it will be a caution to those that is given to lead a wicked and rebellious life like I did into that time ... it is merely to show you all what drinking brings on.

Joseph Meadows was sentenced to hang in front of Worcester Gaol, watched by a large crowd. In the days before the execution the prisoner paid great attention to the ministrations of the chaplain. His brother, two cousins and an uncle all visited him while he awaited trial. However, at his own request, once condemned he had no further family visitors. He did, however, write a letter for his former employer, Mr Rann:

I have for some time past been expecting a letter from you. As I have not received one I could not feel satisfied without writing.

*I trust you have forgiven me for all my past misconduct. As I trust
we shall be forgiven, there is forgiveness for all if we ask of God
believing we shall receive. Although our sins may be as numerous
as the sands upon the ocean shore, they have me forgiven. The
Blood of Christ cleanseth from all sin.*

*Dear Sir, the time will soon come when I shall have to stand
before an earthly judge but I consider that as nothing when I
think how soon I shall have to stand before that Great Tribunal
to give account up to God. Dear friend, if I may so call you. My
prayer is that you and I may meet around the Throne of God in
Heaven. Jesus died that we might live. He has promised in his
Holy Word that who so ever believeth in Him should not perish
but have everlasting life.*

*He has also said in his Holy Word, that the vilest of the vile
may turn and find grace. He has also invited the heavy laden
sinner to come to him that they may find rest for the soul.*

*Dear Friend, I am earnestly seeking that Salvation, I so much
stand in need of to enable me to bear up under all I shall have to
pass through and which will take me safe to Heaven. I trust in
that great day you with myself and all that are near and dear to
us by the likes of nature will meet in that Holy Place where there
is no pain nor parting and where the weary will be forever at rest.
May the Lord have mercy on you and me for Christ sake.*

It is not certain whether Meadows wrote this letter alone, or if
he was assisted by the prison chaplain.

The executioner on 28 July 1855 was William Calcraft.
Whilst climbing the steps to the scaffold Meadows said to
Calcraft 'do it quickly', Calcraft replied 'I will not be a minute'.
During preparations on the scaffold Meadows remained remarkably composed, and he walked to the noose firmly and
without assistance. Calcraft kept his promise and quickly drew
the bolt, which sent Meadows into eternity. He hung for an
hour, as was normal, before being placed in his coffin fully
clothed, and he was later buried within the precincts of the gaol.
This was the first execution preformed at Worcester since 1849,
when Robert Pulley was hanged for the murder of his sweet-
heart. Calcraft was hangman for almost forty years; he preferred
the 'short drop' method of hanging. He worked quickly once

the culprit was on the scaffold with the noose around their neck. Calcraft also carried out the last public execution, which was that of Michael Barrett, a Fenian; who had detonated a barrel of gunpowder outside Clerkenwell Prison in London, killing a number of people.

The murder of Mary Ann Mason was a very sad case; the loss of two young people because of jealousy is never easy to explain. It would be easy to say that in today's society there would be no need for the subterfuge used by Meadows and Mason. The charge faced by Meadows was one of 'Wilful Murder', but today it is sometimes the case that 'Crimes of Passion' are dealt with as manslaughter. By modern standards this crime would still probably have proceeded as a murder trial, given the premeditation, the carrying of weapons both on the morning and the night before.

By the 1830s murder was about the only crime left where the death penalty was given; transportation was in use for many of the crimes formerly attracting the ultimate penalty. Between 1845 and 1854 only an average of nine people per annum were executed, all for murder. This contrasts with the average from 1805 to 1814 when, on average sixty-six people per annum were executed, twenty per cent of those for murder. This situation had a lot to do with Sir Robert Peel who introduced major reforms and rationalised many areas of the law.

St John's Kates Hill, sadly condemned, due to damage caused during the Dudley earthquake of 2002. Mary's grave lies not far from this entrance gate, though is difficult to find. The authors

A defence was put forward that Meadows should not be convicted of the murder, because of his alleged intoxicated state. This defence failed, possibly because the jury heard that Meadows had only drunk one pint of ale that morning. The defence is not appropriate today; the law states that intoxication should not be a defence to a crime.

The *Sailor's Return* no longer exists in Cromwell Street; indeed the street itself is much shorter than it was in the nineteenth century. A map dated 1853 shows St John's Church, with Cromwell Street a long road, one of few in the area. There are no original buildings left, and therefore, no indication of the location of the public house. The church still exists and the headstone is still in the churchyard. The church itself is sadly condemned following severe damage caused during the 'Dudley earthquake' of 2002. The large and sprawling churchyard is becoming overgrown and neglected, many headstones have fallen and broken; repairs to the church building are unlikely owing to the cost, and it is fenced off.

CHAPTER 12

The Murder of Eliza Bowen 1869

During the early months of 1869, well before the terror in White-chapel, another 'Ripper' committed at least one comparable crime in the Darlaston/Wednesbury area of the Black Country. The case would result in what some would consider to be a serious miscarriage of justice, and the possible release of a sadistic killer back into the community, despite there being seemingly overwhelming evidence against him.

At 7 am on Sunday 28 February 1869 John Turner, an ostler employed by the Patent Shaft and Axle Company, found the mutilated body of Eliza Bowen. The discovery was made in Mud Lane, Wednesbury, a make-shift road running from Hall End to the Darlaston turnpike. The corpse was lying in a field at the side of the road. Just at the moment Turner noticed the body he saw Henry Clay, the local lamplighter, approaching the scene.

Both men entered the field to more closely examine the woman's body and almost immediately realised the horror of what they had found. Clay went straight away to notify the police. Superintendent Holland attended the scene, in company with PCs Walters and Evans. A crowd had already gathered, attracted by Clay's cries of 'murder'. A brief examination of the corpse was carried out at the scene before the body was taken to the *Blue Ball Inn*, Hall End in Wednesbury. Bowen was clearly dead and cold, she was covered with dirt, and the few clothes she wore were torn and disordered.

The inquest took place at the public house with the District Coroner, Mr Edwin Hooper, officiating. Mr Kerr was the surgeon who carried out the post-mortem. The jury was drawn from the local area, Mr Mayers, a local butcher, was the foreman. Mr Kerr stated that the body was

... in a horrible condition, had been subjected to revolting treatment. She had been violated and sixteen pieces of furnace cinder and a brick had been forced into her body, causing her death.

Evidence given by the police was that there had been very clear signs of a violent struggle in a ditch about twenty-five yards from where the body was found. The woman's body had been dragged from the place where the murder had occurred and thrown down an embankment, where she had been found. She had put up a great struggle and had probably cried out before she died. Unfortunately the nearest house was 150 yards away, and at the estimated time of the attack there was a violent thunderstorm, which would have meant any cries would go unheard.

One piece of evidence that proved vital was a piece of cloth torn from a muffler. This had a distinctive pattern, and it was found near to the body. There were great hopes that this would help the police in their enquiries. Some footmarks were also noted, though there had been much contamination of the scene owing to the number of people who had walked over it.

Eliza Bowen was aged fifty and lived at The Green in Darlaston. She was well-known to her neighbours as a 'drunken drab' hardly sober from one weekend to the next. Her husband, William Bowen, was serving a nine-month prison sentence in Stafford Gaol for fowl-stealing. Their son William Bowen, an underhand puddler had left home some months earlier because of his mother's depraved habits. His brother had also been sent to a Reformatory six months before. It was her son William who identified his mother's body.

Proper examination of the body took place at the *Blue Ball*. Mr Kerr noted that Bowen's genital organs were swollen and covered with coagulated blood. There had been a piece of stone pushed into her rectum, a further sixteen pieces had been forced into her vagina. He considered that the immediate cause of death was the insertion of these stones. Further examination revealed another large piece of stone pushed deep into her rectum. When asked if these had been inserted before or after death, Mr Kerr replied that Bowen was almost certainly alive

The Blue Ball *as it looks today.* The authors

when this foul deed was done, as there was much inflammation of her rectum and genitals.

Police enquiries into the murder quickly led them to a man named William Hall, aged forty-two, who had been seen with the deceased on the night of the murder. A search of his home at Kings Hill near Darlaston, revealed a muffler; this was seized and compared with the piece of cloth found at the scene. The torn piece found at the scene fitted exactly with the rest of the muffler.

Hall was a striker at Messrs Slater and Rubery (Iron Bridge and Girder Manufacturers) in Darlaston. He was arrested from his place of work and appeared agitated and pale. An identity parade was quickly arranged and four other men stood alongside Hall. Mrs Eliza Reader picked him out as someone she had seen with the deceased. Despite the evidence Hall denied being involved in the crime. Further evidence was found to implicate Hall; there were dried patches of soil on his clothing, which matched that found in Mud Lane. Hall was also a man of bad character, his first wife left him and another woman he lived with was forced into the Workhouse Infirmary. Since she left him Hall had married a second time.

Questioning of the suspect was the responsibility of Sergeant Steele. He asked Hall if he had been to the *Victoria*, the *Manchester* or the *Fourpenny House* on the night of the murder. Hall admitted he had visited those pubs, but claimed to have been alone. Two witnesses, Charles Orton and Joseph Burford claimed to have seen Hall, with the victim, at 9.30 pm in the *Victoria Inn*, Walsall Road, Darlaston. Hall was given the opportunity of cross-examining Burford, who described in detail his sighting of Hall and Bowen, but he asked no questions of Burford.

Further witnesses put Hall and Eliza together at the *Dragon Inn*, Wednesbury, and the *Horse and Jockey* at 11.30 pm. A waiter at the *Dragon*, John Pynn, gave evidence of the behaviour of both Eliza and Hall. They had been drinking from the same jug and Eliza had dropped it and caused a chip. She was ordered out when she said she had no money to pay for the damage. As they left Hall picked up the jug and smashed it on the floor.

Eliza Reader, the person who had picked out Hall in the identity parade, was walking home with her husband Charles. They were on their way home to Darlaston Green from her mother's in Earps Lane, Wednesbury at about 12.30 am. In Mud Lane they saw the accused in the shadows with a woman. This was at a point near to Hall End, rather than the turnpike end of Mud Lane. Charles said 'Ode fella, you've got a tidy nerve to have a woman here at this time of night'; neither replied and both appeared tipsy.

The case was then adjourned for a week, on Hall's return a large crowd gathered outside Wednesbury Police Court. When the case resumed an eleven-year-old boy gave evidence. Jonah Dutton of Hall End had been sent to fetch a quart of ale from

George Lloyds' beer house in High Street. In Trouse Lane he saw Hall and Eliza, she was trying to walk along the turnpike to Darlaston, and he was trying to persuade her to walk towards Mud Lane. Samuel Kendrick also saw a couple staggering into Mud Lane just after midnight. He described the man's clothes as a billycock hat, a dark jacket and light trousers. Charles Orton was recalled to the box and gave evidence of clothing that matched that of Kendrick. He also described a muffler worn by Hall. There was a denial from Hall that he had been wearing the muffler.

Mud Lane no longer exists, and was just a footpath at the time of the incident. The Darlaston Turnpike is shown on a 1902 map of the area, as is Hall End and Trouse Lane. The place the body was found was near to Park Street, where Eliza Ellis had heard two men urging a woman to go with them. My 'best guess' is that Mud Lane was somewhere just below Cow Pasture Colliery on the map below, to the left of Hall End. The scene would have been near to the *Blue Ball*, where Eliza was taken for the inquest.

Further evidence was given by a number of witnesses, who all claimed Hall had owned and worn a distinctive muffler over a period of time. Hannah Wilks lived next door to Hall and saw the muffler on the washing line on the Monday morning after

Map of the area, Mud Lane is thought to have been just below Cow Pasture Colliery. The area is now built up and bears no resemblance to its appearance in 1869. The authors

the murder. She noticed that the end was torn off it. Police evidence was given that the muffler (minus the torn piece) was found at Hall's home, on comparing the torn piece it exactly fitted the rest of the muffler.

Against this seemingly overwhelming amount of evidence against him Hall maintained he was innocent. Apart from being the worse for drink Hall claimed Eliza was alive and well when they parted. The only real glimmer of hope for him came in the shape of Mrs Eliza Ellis of Park Street. She said that, just before the storm she was awake attending to a sick child, she heard several men were trying to 'induce a woman' using filthy language.

Having heard all this evidence against Hall, but before hearing any witnesses Mrs Hall claimed would attend and give their depositions, the magistrates committed Hall to the July Assize court, and remanded him to Stafford Gaol until that hearing. This decision would have serious implications for the progress of this case. Hall was then transported by train to Stafford; a large crowd witnessed his removal to the railway station by police officers.

Mrs Hall claimed she was not aware that she was expected to arrange for defence witnesses to be present at the next hearing. The court, however, was adamant that the prisoner and his wife had been told of this expectation.

The coroner's inquest had not yet decided on the manner of death of Eliza Bowen. The coroner wanted the jury to return a verdict of 'wilful murder' and name Hall as the man responsible. However, to do this Hall needed to be present in court, as there was fresh evidence to be put to the inquest including the evidence of defence witnesses. The difficulty arose because Hall had already been committed to the Assize court, meaning there was no power to produce him to the inquest. Even when the coroner had an interview with the Home Secretary, Sir Adolphus Liddell, there was no resolution. There was a promise to review the law once this case was concluded.

A further adjournment and an affidavit from Hall brought the matter no closer to resolution. It was likely that fresh evidence would be brought against Hall, he was not permitted to be present to hear this evidence, and the Home Secretary did not have the power to order his production, even a judge in Chambers was unable to secure Hall's appearance at court. The inquest was again adjourned to the end of May.

On re-opening the inquest on 27 May 1869 Hall was still not produced. The jury indicated an 'open' verdict would have to be returned. This would have severe implications for the Assize Court in July. Not surprisingly the Grand Jury at Stafford had no option but to find 'no true bill' against Hall, which meant he was held innocent in the eyes of the law, and released from custody. A newspaper reporter said:

I say nothing as to whether the evidence was sufficient or insufficient to convict the accused man; he is now in the eye of the law, and must be held by the world innocent of the crime with which he was charged.

The verdict of the Grand Jury came as a great surprise to local people in Darlaston. There had been much press coverage of the case, sometimes with graphic detail about how Bowen lost her life. It was difficult to comprehend why the magistrates thought there was sufficient evidence to commit Hall for trial, yet there was no case to answer at the Assize Court.

The Grand Jury had a sole purpose at this time, they would hear the prosecution evidence, which seeks to prove the Bill of Indictment and decide whether or not there was sufficient evidence to prove a *prima facie* case for the Assize Court to hear. The institution was also a shield against unfounded and oppressive prosecution. If the indictment was not proved to the satisfaction of at least twelve of the grand Jurors (the Grand Jury was usually at least twenty-three strong) then the Bill would be endorsed 'Ignoramus' or 'No true bill' and the case dismissed. The defence had no part to play in the Grand Jury System, only prosecution evidence was heard.

This safety net still exists today, but in a different form. The defence in a jury trial can now make application to the judge that the prosecution has not made out a 'Prime facie' case to answer on behalf of the defendant. The judge then makes that decision and can dismiss the charges. This rarely happens because of checks put into place by the Crown Prosecution

Service, who ensure that the evidence is strong enough to proceed to trial and sufficient to have a strong likelihood of success at court, the 'evidential sufficiency criteria'. Where cases fail for lack of evidence is usually when crucial witnesses fail to attend court, or make significant departures from their written statements when giving evidence or being cross examined.

Following the abortive trial of Hall, there was then a series of confessions to the murder, which succeeded in muddying the water. Firstly, James Owen confessed at Sutton Coldfield that he had committed the murder, he later withdrew his statement. Then nineteen years later, in the *Worcestershire Advertiser* dated 14 April 1888 William Clifford (then aged thirty-five) was reported as having made a confession at Stratford Petty Session (in Essex). Clifford stated that he had feloniously killed and murdered a woman some eighteen years ago on a cinder bank near Wolverhampton, near where he lived in Stafford Street. Clifford went into Leytonstone Police Station and made his confession to Inspector John Walsh. He was given the caution and a written statement was then taken from him, this being his statement:

I, William Clifford, murdered a woman between the hours of four and six in the morning on a cinder bank near Wolverhampton, in Staffordshire, about eighteen years ago. My sister, Sarah Knight, who resided in Burslem, in the Potteries, North Staffordshire, knows all about it. Though it will break my mother's heart, I want to have it cleared up so I can have a clear mind.

Clifford later went on to withdraw his confession, claiming that he had been out of work for six weeks and must have been drunk at the time of his statement. Inspector Walsh stated that Clifford was sober at the time and was sent to the House of Detention to examine his state of mind. There is no evidence that Clifford ever stood trial, possibly because he was declared insane. The case of the murder of Eliza Bowen remains unsolved today.

By one newspaper account Eliza Bowen was the third victim of an attack in the Mud Lane area. The first was twenty-seven-year-old Ann Proctor who was attacked on 7 January 1869 and a month later Sarah Mullett, who was in her early twenties was also attacked. Both had their mouths stuffed with clay by a tall, dark man. The first victim had 'Jezebel' carved into her forehead and the second the letter 'J'. There is no mention of either of these attacks in contemporary newspapers, or in any archive material that I have read.

CHAPTER 13

The Alvechurch Murder 1885

Worcestershire Constabulary lost one of their officers between 2.15 and 8 am on 28 February 1885. PC James Davies was thirty-three years old and he was stationed at Beoley on the borders of the Black Country. James had worked in the Alvechurch area for about eight years. His police career started in 1875 when he joined the Kidderminster Police Force, where he worked for about two years. He left in 1877 when his wife inherited a large sum of money. Davies was induced to set up in business as a 'General Dealer' in High Street, Stourport, but this business failed, and was eventually sold. PC Davies then joined Worcestershire Constabulary. James was very well respected, both at Kidderminster and Stourport, and he was well known as a total abstainer of alcohol.

On the night of his murder PC Davies was working a regular night-shift beat. Contact with officers working beats was by pre-arranged meetings at beat borders. Another Wythall officer, and close friend of James, PC Whitehouse, was the last person to see PC Davies when they met at their appointed time at 2.15 am PC Davies then headed towards Stecham Farm, for his next appointment at 4 am with PC Sheppard of Alvechurch, but Sheppard was at home ill so PC Davies was not missed. Farm labourer, John Twigg of Rowley Green raised the alarm at 8 am that he had discovered the body of PC Davies in Icknield Street near Weatheroak Hill. John was on his way to work in Weatheroak; the body was lying in a pool of blood with over forty stab wounds; his head had almost been severed. The nearest farm was Newbould Farm; the only information gleaned from there was that the dog barked between 3.30 and 4 am.

Superintendent Tyler from Kings Heath attended the scene and commenced an investigation. A twin set of footprints led back from the body to the gate of a nearby farmer, then a single set from the farm gate to the hen-house. Plaster casts were made of the two sets of footprints, one set fitted the boots of PC Davies, and the other set would become relevant later on. PC Davies's hands bore very severe defence-cut wounds from the vicious assault. There was also a gash across his throat, which had proved to be the fatal wound. The officers' whistle and oak stick were found 200 yards from his body, and his handcuffs were still in his pocket.

On checking his stock the farmer discovered that six of his hens were missing, it would appear that PC Davies had caught a poacher red-handed. The immediate suspect was Moses Shrimpton, the terror of Eastern Worcestershire. Shrimpton was a regular thief in the area and his hatred of the police was well known. A feud had existed for some between Shrimpton and PC Davies. Shrimpton was an extremely violent man who had served seven years' penal servitude for attacking a police officer; he had also previously brutally attacked a gamekeeper. It will never be known if PC Davies planned to target a poacher, or if he came across him during his patrol and surprised him.

The investigation moved quickly, James had been wearing a watch, bought in Stourport; this had been taken from his body. This watch was traced to George Facer, a maltster, of 9 Dartmouth Street, Birmingham. He was arrested as an accessory after the murder. Shrimpton's photographs had been circulated in Birmingham at Duke Street police station, and as a result of this an officer recognised him as someone who lodged at 9 Bartholomew Street with Mary Ann Morton, a forty-year-old woman, known locally as 'mad Mary'. Morton had a set of criminal convictions to match those of Shrimpton; her pedigree consisted mainly of theft, assault and prostitution. Both were known to frequent some of the roughest taverns in the town. The couple were easy to find, they were arrested on the day after the murder, Shrimpton had cuts to his face and Mary was in possession of a large knife with two blades.

All three prisoners appeared at Balsall Heath (Worcestershire) Police Court; they were charged and remanded in custody, Shrimpton with the murder, Morton as an accessory after the fact, and Facer with handling the watch. Colonel

Kingswinford Library

www.better.org.uk/Kingswinford
Tel: 01384 812740

Borrowed Items : 17/11/2021   14:15
Customer ID: ********7499

Loaned today

Title: Dead end
Due back: 15/12/2021

Title. Foul deeds and suspicious deaths around
the Black Country
Due back: 15/12/2021

Total item(s) loaned today: 2
Previous Amount Owed: 0.00 GBP
Overdue: 0
Reservation(s) pending: 0
Reservation(s) to collect: 0
Total item(s) on loan: 4

Items you already have on loan
house of the hanged woman
Due back: 15/12/2021
Pardonable lies
Due back: 15/12/2021

Carmichael, Chief Constable of Worcestershire, explained that the clothes seized from Shrimpton had been forwarded to Doctor Stevenson, of Guy's Hospital for analysis. It was believed that there was much blood on the clothing, and that it would take a week for the results of the analysis. A further application was granted for Shrimpton to be remanded for a week and for him to be removed to Alvechurch to be present at the inquest.

A crucial piece of evidence was the boot print taken from the scene, this matched perfectly with the footwear worn by Shrimpton. A vain hope was held by Shrimpton that Morton would provide him with an alibi. The stakes proved too high for Mary, she told police that Shrimpton had been out for the whole of the previous night, and on his return had attempted to wash blood out of his clothes and hat.

Moses Shrimpton was sixty-five at the time of the murder; a father of two sons and two daughters, the youngest child being twenty-five years old. Moses was born in 1819 in a farm cottage near Redditch, and learned his 'tickle' at an early age following the death of his father. In and around Tardebigge his skills were put to use very quickly feeding his mother and a number of brothers and sisters. He was to continue to steal during the remainder of his life. He would be described today as a 'career criminal'. Shrimpton had a lengthy criminal record whose convictions included poaching and hen-stealing and there was a photograph of him on his record at Worcestershire County Police Headquarters.

Recently released from gaol, Shrimpton had served time at both Winson Green prison in Birmingham and Worcester gaol on numerous occasions. It was reported that he was not a model prisoner, and whilst in custody he had spent long periods on the 'treadmill' and 'the crank', both methods of torture which often resulted in the death of inmates. A measure of his strength and tenacity, Shrimpton survived, but was turned into a hump-backed, bow-legged man and was described by a contemporary reporter as being 'more ape-like than human'. Shrimpton had only recently been released from gaol.

The trial took place at Worcester Assizes on 7 May 1885, before Baron Huddleston. The verdict seemed to be inevitable;

he was convicted and sentenced to death. It is said that, after his previous term of imprisonment, he had spoken of being willing to die rather than face further incarceration in Winson Green. Cynically there did not appear to be an option of him not committing further crimes, so maybe his death sentence, and possibly the death of anyone who may get in his way was inevitable.

Justice was done, and was seen to be done much more quickly than it is today. Less than three months after committing his horrific murder, on Whit Monday, 25 May 1885. Moses Shrimpton was put to death by hanging in Worcester. A last minute attempt for a stay of execution because of the Bank Holiday was turned down by Home Secretary Godfrey Lushington. Ironically Lushington was an advocate of penal reform, his views were expressed when he gave evidence to a Government committee on the penal system:

I regard as unfavourable to reformation the status of a prisoner throughout his whole career; the crushing of self-respect, the starving of all moral instinct he may possess, the absence of all opportunity to do or receive a kindness, the continual association with none but criminal . . . I believe the true mode of reforming a man or restoring him to society is exactly in the opposite direction of all these; but, of course, this is a mere idea. It is quite impracticable in a prison. In fact the unfavourable features I have mentioned are inseparable from prison life.

Had his views been acted upon in earlier times, the cycle of Shrimpton's commission of crime and time spent in prison may have been curtailed, and his life may have been completely different. Unfortunately, this was not the case, although it is well known that prison, in terms of reforming people who are incarcerated, still does not work, with a large proportion of offenders returning to crime after release from prison.

Whilst awaiting his fate at Worcester, Shrimpton apparently became repentant, paying great attention whenever the Chaplain, the Reverend A Telfer, visited. Shrimpton also spent considerable time reading the bible. Reverend Telfer was impressed by the demeanour of the prisoner; he noted that Shrimpton seemed more sensible of his fate as the time of his execution neared. He expressed a desire to see his children; accordingly his son and son-in-law had a farewell interview with him on Saturday, two days before the execution. The meeting was quite upsetting for Shrimpton, but he said nothing about his crime. On Sunday, a woman believed to be Mary Morton, called at the prison with a man said to be her husband, asking to see the prisoner; they were turned away. Shrimpton spent most of his last day with the chaplain.

James Berry was England's executioner from 1884 to 1891. He was a former police officer in the Wakefield West Riding Police in Yorkshire from 1874 to 1882. He met through a mutual friend, William Marwood, a cobbler and part-time executioner. Berry was a man of mystery and took a genuine interest in both the criminals he despatched and the crimes they committed. Shrimpton was to be Berry's nineteenth execution. His most famous previous 'execution' was that of John Babbacombe Lee 'the man they could not hang' at Exeter in February 1885. When Berry pulled the lever on the gallows nothing happened. After three attempts, as was the law, Lee was reprieved. The problem on that occasion was that Berry had not tested the apparatus before the execution.

Berry observed that Shrimpton was 'a man of strong character and much determination of purpose, a leader amongst the ruffians of his district'. He also compared this execution with that of John Lee. As an old man Shrimpton's weight was difficult to judge, and Berry described the last gruesome moments of his life:

I pulled the lever, and above the tolling of the prison bells the thud of the doors was heard, and Moses Shrimpton disappeared from view.

Shrimpton walked the forty yards to the scaffold with a firm step. The Governor, surgeon, chaplain, two magistrates and the under-sheriff accompanied him. Shrimpton was asked if he had anything to say, and replied 'no'. Berry adjusted the rope, and placed the white cap over his face. He then stood aside and gave the signal on the stroke of eight o'clock. Shrimpton disappeared from view; the nine-foot drop given to Shrimpton tore open his throat and caused his head to almost be completely severed from his body. His death was instantaneous, painless and a legal execution and there was no real criticism at the inquest that followed. This was not the first mistake by Berry, and it was not to be his last.

James Berry carried out his last four executions in August 1891, three on consecutive days. His final execution was his 131st at Winchester. This was of Edward Henry Fawcett, who shot his estranged wife four times. On 4 March 1892 Berry wrote to Home Secretary, the Right Honourable Henry Matthews tendering his resignation. He cited interference in his 130th execution by the Doctor who recommended the length of the drop. This lead to a similar near decapitation as in the Moses Shrimpton case, this time however, the Press and the coroner's inquest were not so kind to him.

Berry's career deeply affected him; he went from being teetotal to admitting consuming brandy before he carried out his executions. Once out of his role as executioner he embarked on a lecture tour supporting the abolition of capital punishment. This was not a success and he wrote on several occasions to Prison Commissioners to be re-instated as hangman. He attempted suicide and suffered from depression. Eventually he was rescued and turned to religion; he became an evangelical preacher and died in 1913.

PC Davies is buried in Beoley churchyard, only a couple of miles from the scene of his murder. His marble headstone is still in good condition today. Following the incident a sandstone plaque was placed in Icknield Street at the point where his body was found. Over the years this deteriorated and has been replaced with a simple concrete one. Try as I might I cannot find the exact spot where the plaque was located. The lane is very narrow, and runs down Weatheroak Hill towards Beoley. I could imagine the scene, pitch-black, very remote, and the officer alone when he confronted Shrimpton as he left the scene of his crime. It is not known whether PC Davies came upon Shrimpton during his patrol, or if he had followed him for some time, suspecting him of no good. However, the two met that night, the result was that a police officer lost his life for the price of six chickens.

Beoley Church where James Davies is buried. The authors

The scale of the tragedy was felt across the region. PC Davies had three young children, and his widow was expecting a fourth. There was much public sympathy for the family. His widow was granted a gratuity of £60 18s 8d, the maximum allowed. A local newspaper in Kidderminster recognised the duty PC Davies performed:

> *It is the duty of the public to see that the family neither starve nor has to seek the obnoxious workhouse. As a public servant, he met his death because he would not shirk his duty, and he has thereby proved himself a greater hero than the man who rushes into danger merely for the excitement it affords or the questionable honours he may gain.*

The divisional Sergeant at Stourport, Sergeant Oliver, took an active interest in raising funds for the Davies family. In Dudley there were further collections for PC Davies. Chief Superintendent Burton wrote to the *Dudley Herald* and invited

The well-preserved grave of James Davies; it seems he still has visitors to his final resting place.
The authors

contributions from the people of Dudley for a fund. The generous public appeals for his dependants raised a much larger total of money. This included £5 from the Bishop of Worcester, as well as the results of collections from workers in the carpet industry, and donations from the Mayor of Dudley, D Howat and other notable citizens from the town.

There was a story told that Shrimpton wrote a confession to the murder, which was apparently found in his snuffbox. There was a further suggestion that PC Davies was killed by two poachers, this was never substantiated, and indeed the description of the footprints around the scene could only mean one attacker.

CHAPTER 14

The Wyrley Gang and the Case of George Edalji 1903

In the late nineteenth century no series of crimes generated so much speculation as the series of murders by 'Jack the Ripper' in 1888. Even in the twenty-first century books and articles still appear, with new theories and seemingly new evidence to identify 'Jack'. Back in 1903, in the village of Great Wyrley, on the northern edge of the Black Country another 'Ripper' went to work. His victims were not prostitutes; they were not even human, but the effect on the local community was akin to events of fifteen years previous in Whitechapel.

In 1903 the small Staffordshire village of Great Wyrley with a population of 5,000 had its own scare and brought back to the mind the legend of Jack the Ripper. Someone was maiming horses and other animals and for a time there was no clue as to who was responsible. The first incident took place on 1 February 1903 with the slaughter of a horse belonging to a local farmer, Joseph Holmes. The horse was found in a field; the injuries inflicted on the animal shocked locals. The assumption was that whoever did this bore a grudge against Holmes. This theory was discounted a few weeks later at Easter, on Sunday, 12 April, when a second horse was found with even more horrific injuries in a field abutting Walsall Road, Great Wyrley, at Loggerheads Farm.

The local village constable called in extra officers to assist when locals become frightened to leave their homes after dark. Inspector Campbell from Cannock was put in charge of the case, assisted by Sergeant Parsons from Great Wyrley. The mutilations continued throughout the summer, in the seven months between February and August a total of five horses, three cows and a number of sheep were attacked. Then began a series of frightening letters. Each letter was signed 'Captain Darby' and the writer boasted that 'he would not stop at horses'. The lives and property of several local families were threatened, and then pranks began. Coal was delivered which had not been ordered; a horse and cart arrived at a home to take the occupant 'to the asylum'; and even undertakers received messages about funerals for people who were still alive.

Initial indications were that a gang was carrying out the crimes, but the police believed a single person of unsound mind to be responsible. The investigations initially focussed on the letters, the style was that of an uneducated person, but hand-writing experts believed this was deliberate to try and confuse the police, whose efforts to catch 'The Wyrley Ripper' was so far unsuccessful.

Then police had a break in the case. They received anony-mous information concerning the son of the vicar of Great Wyrley, George Edalji. George was the eldest son of Shapurji Edalji and Charlotte Stoneham. George, a former pupil at Walsall Grammar School, was a qualified solicitor, and had been an outstanding student, with an office at 54 Newhall Street, Birmingham. He was a well educated young man who took little part in local life. George had very poor eyesight; he was myopic and this was combined with astigmatism.

Shapurji was a Parsee and had been the Vicar at Great Wyrley since December 1875. The Parsee was, at the time, the oldest established Asian people in Britain. They had been dubbed the 'Jews of India' – dominating the commercial life of Victorian Bombay. The best known modern-day Parsee was Freddie Mercury, late vocalist of rock group Queen. The Parsee had always enjoyed high moral standing in India; they were renowned for their honesty and philanthropy.

Charlotte Stoneham had strong links with the church at Great Wyrley, before her husband took over; her uncle had been Vicar at Great Wyrley for twenty-six years. The Edalji family had had problems in the village; they had previously received hoax letters in 1888 and again in a series of letters lasting from 1892–95. The Chief Constable of Staffordshire Captain George Augustus Anson was public in his views of the family; he 'thought Black Men less than beasts'. Anson believed

54 Newhall Street, Birmingham, the offices where George Edalji practiced as a solicitor.
The authors

George was responsible for the letters. Locals did not like the thought of a black man marrying a white woman.

The anonymous information named George as the Great Wyrley Ripper. On 18 August 1903 police visited the vicarage. A red-roan pit-pony had been found bleeding in a field that morning. No one was seen in and around the scene of the crime, but the police, acting on the anonymous tip, went to the vicarage in search of the evidence. The police investigation initially consisted of a search of the vicarage grounds, this produced a bloodstained razor and a coat. Police went quickly to George's office in Newhall Street Birmingham. George admitted he had worn the coat at breakfast that morning and he was quickly arrested on suspicion of the crime. The police investigation of George's alleged crime was swift, and within a few hours he had been charged and remanded in custody.

On 19 August, the day after his arrest, George appeared before magistrates who remanded him for two weeks for committal proceedings. On his next appearance he was committed for trial at Staffordshire Quarter Sessions. George was remanded in custody until the start of his trial on 20 October 1903.

A number of factors weighed heavily against George at the time of his trial. There was considerable feeling in the area about this series of crimes. The police, up until the arrest of George, had been baffled by the outrages, and they were very anxious to bring someone to justice. This undue haste had been fuelled by the comments of the Chief Constable, who was public about his views on the Edalji family. The odds of George receiving a fair trial were also stacked by the apparent imperative within the criminal justice system that someone had to be quickly 'bought to book' for this series of crimes. Finally, there was the introduction into the evidence of the anonymous letters, yet with very little in the way of evidence that George had written the letters.

Once George became a suspect the police investigation revolved solely around finding evidence to convict him. This ran contrary to the principles of our Criminal Justice system: to find the person responsible for the crime. The style of investigation adopted by Inspector Campbell and his men was more appropriate for countries such as France, who work to a more rigorous 'crime control' system of justice, where a suspect is guilty until he proves his innocence. In Great Britain the justice system should reflect 'due process'. This sometimes means that the guilty go free, but that miscarriages of justice should be eliminated, as there are safeguards in the way the police operate. Examples that the police were not 'playing by the rules' were many. Once George became a suspect the vicarage fell under continuous watch by the police, and once the latest offence was discovered officers went straight to the vicarage.

At the trial the cards were stacked against George being treated fairly. The police and others were set on convicting him, at the cost of true justice. The police evidence contained both inconsistencies and also contradictions. For example, there were two officers posted to watch the field where the latest crime occurred, and neither of those officers was called to give evidence.

Two sergeants involved in the policing operation gave contradictory testimony. Sergeant Robinson stated that the vicarage was under observations; Sergeant Parsons on the other hand said it was not. There were more inconsistencies in the police evidence, this time involving Inspector Campbell, the man originally assigned to 'manage' the investigation. He gave evidence about the razor found at the vicarage and said it was wet at the time it was found; he made no mention of horse hairs on the razor. Sergeant Parsons, on the other hand, said one or two horse hairs had stuck to the razor. He also insisted Inspector Campbell showed the razor to the Edalji family.

At the trial there were two main threads of evidence; circumstantial and the evidence of the anonymous letters that had been written about the offences. The circumstantial evidence alone was not enough to convict George, and consisted of items seized from the vicarage on the morning of 18 August. There was the suit of clothes, with muddy trousers and a damp jacket and waistcoat; the trousers however were not seized by the police, and therefore not examined. There was a very muddy pair of boots, one of which was immediately seized, the other collected later.

Stafford Shire Hall, where Stafford Assizes were held. The authors

The police made only limited use of this evidence. They stated that hairs found on the waistcoat were horse hairs, and also claimed to have shown this evidence to the family; they denied they were shown any hairs. The boots could have provided good forensic evidence, but again this opportunity was missed. Only rough comparison was made with footprints in the field, and there appeared to be no attempt to link the mud on the boots or the mud on the trousers, with soil from the field where the latest crime had occurred.

The second thread of the trial pertained to the letters; these were shown to the jury at the trial. It appears that the jurors were persuaded to believe that George was responsible for writing them, and made the assumption that the writer had also committed the crimes. The letters made statements about the outrages, and alleged guilt against a number of local men, including George.

There was also another hurdle for the prosecution to overcome; one that today might have thrown enough doubt on the veracity of the case for it to have been dropped. On 21 September 1903, whilst George was in custody, on remand, another incident occurred. A horse belonging to local man Harry Green of High House Farm, Great Wyrley was found butchered, with its stomach slashed open. Green admitted doing it himself, to dispose of a horse that was old and of no value. If this was the case why did Green go out at night and mutilate a horse when many more humane methods existed? An investigation followed, but the police took Green's confession as true, after all if they didn't then it completely undermined their case against George Edalji.

During the trial it was alleged that George was operating as part of a gang, with other members being responsible for the latest outrage. After four days the jury retired to consider their verdict. They returned and found George 'guilty' of an offence under the Malicious Damage Act of 1861. The judge sentenced George to seven years penal servitude. George had been found guilty on the flimsiest of evidence, hearsay, circumstantial, tainted 'forensic' evidence. This case was a shocking example of British injustice.

There was then another twist in the tale, Sir Arthur Conan Doyle, creator of Sherlock Holmes, began to highlight what he perceived to be a great injustice. Doyle had read about the case in an article in an obscure paper called the *Umpire*, sent to him by George. In the spring of 1906 he arrived in Great Wyrley to begin an investigation worthy of his creation. The results appeared as a series of articles in the *Daily Telegraph* and insisted that a grave miscarriage of justice had occurred. Conan Doyle in his *Memories and Adventures* commented that:

> The evidence was incredibly weak, and yet the police, all pulling together and twisting all things to their end, managed to get a conviction.

The author carried out the journey from the vicarage to the scene of the crime. George would have had to pass over the L&NW railway and negotiate a small gap in the thick hedge; the field was about three-quarters of a mile from the vicarage. This trail would have had to have been negotiated by the nearly blind man during the hours of darkness. Always willing to dramatise,

Conan Doyle described the journey as 'an obstacle course worthy of Odysseus'.

The evidence was compelling: George's eyesight was a major factor; he was unable to recognise his father from a distance of six feet. This seemed incongruous when compared to the reality of the crimes George was convicted of. 'The Ripper' would have had to negotiate marshy fields, circumvent dense thorn hedges and climbed high walls, all in total darkness, to commit them. On one occasion a mutilated horse had been dragged 140 yards from the place of the crime to the doorstep of the owner. Conan Doyle was determined that justice would be done and George pardoned for the crimes. As part of his investigation Conan Doyle sent George to see an eminent eye specialist in London, who confirmed both his astigmatism and myopia.

Almost 10,000 people, including many respected members of the legal profession, signed a petition demanding the release of George, organised by Conan Doyle. It led to release from prison on 19 October 1906 on a 'ticket of leave' – supervised by the police. He had served nearly three years of his sentence, he received however, not one penny in compensation for the time wrongly spent in prison. The proceeds of a fund set up by the *Daily Telegraph*, a total of £300, was given to George.

Meanwhile, in and around Great Wyrley the 'Ripper' continued to commit gruesome crimes. Both maiming of animals and writing of letters continued, Brook House Farm was the scene of several killings of cows, sheep and horses. Police enquires continued, and another local man fell under suspicion – Thomas Farrington a collier who had worked in a slaughter-house in his youth. Once, when drunk, he bragged he was 'The Ripper'; this boast was to lead to an appearance at Stafford Quarter Sessions where he received a sentence of three years penal servitude. Once again, the police appeared to have arrested the wrong man, as there was more maiming and more letters from 'Captain Darby'. This time though there was no quest for justice from Conan Doyle and since the jailing of Farrington no further arrests were made by the police. The identity of 'The Ripper' remains a mystery.

The Edalji case was to have wider implications for the Criminal Justice System in England and Wales. Home

Sir Arthur Conan Doyle. Authors' collection

Secretary Gladstone set up a committee to look into the circumstances. Sir Arthur Wilson, John Lloyd Wharton and Sir Albert
de Rutzen (Chief Magistrate) examined the case. Rutzen was
a second cousin of Staffordshire Chief Constable George
Augustus Anson, though the Home Office did not believe this
compromised the enquiry. On 23 April 1907 they found that

the conviction was unsatisfactory, and disagreed with the findings of the jury. They found that the conviction should not have occurred, although they seemed to persist in believing that Edalji himself wrote the letters, and therefore, brought some of his problems on himself. They were also keen not to apportion any blame on the Home Secretaries who had made decisions regarding the case. Edalji was re-admitted to the Law Society, thereby allowing him to practice again as a solicitor. The case and Conan Doyle's exposure of this obvious miscarriage of justice would help in the establishing of the Criminal Court of Appeal in 1907.

The 'Captain Darby' letters would continue for many years, leading to the arrest in 1934 of Enoch Knowles from Wednesbury. Knowles admitted writing the letters and was also sent to prison. There is also some suggestion that Conan Doyle identified a strong suspect, someone who could have written the letters, including threatening letters to Conan Doyle himself. He identified a link back to Walsall Grammar School, and interviewed the headmaster, who named Royston Sharp, who had been expelled from the school for disorderly conduct. Sharp was a trainee butcher in Great Wyrley. Conan Doyle was unable to name the man during his investigation due to the libel laws, and his name only came to light after Sharp's death.

CHAPTER 15

Caroline in the Cornfield 1906

What did the events of the early hours of Wednesday, 27 June 1906 have to do with the discovery, two weeks later, of the badly decomposed body of Caroline Pearson? In the early hours of that fatal morning Emma Cox was savagely attacked by Enoch, her estranged husband; they had been married five years. Caroline was found in a rye field, about fifteen yards from a public footpath; passers by had been alerted by the awful smell coming from within the field.

Enoch and Emma Cox were both twenty-four-years-old, and had lived unhappily for almost all of their married life, with Enoch's father Solomon, in High Town, Cradley Heath. They had two children who were three and five years old respectively at the time of the incident. A third child, born only a few weeks prior to these events, lived for only nine hours.

By all accounts Enoch was a good worker, he was a chain-maker, as were many people from the area, and worked for Walkers in Netherton. Enoch was also one for the ladies, and, when drunk, would frequently assault his wife. Emma was also a chain-maker; she worked in a chain shop at the bottom of the garden where they lived. About seven weeks before 22 June Emma left her husband and went to live with her parents in Newtown, Cradley Heath. She actually slept two doors away at the house of a neighbour named Priest. The two children stayed with their father, and Enoch employed a woman called Emma Brooks, from Brierley Hill, to look after the children. Enoch was soon co-habiting with Brooks. Emma was constantly pestered by Enoch to return home, and the local police were called on several occasions to deal with him when matters got out of hand. Enoch had also sent his father to plead with Emma to come home, without success.

Events came to a head between Enoch and Emma on the evening of Tuesday 26 June, when Enoch paid Emma a last visit. What his intentions might have been will be explored later, but what is fairly certain is that this was a 'make or break' meeting. Enoch, on finding the door open, entered the house and confronted Emma, stating 'come on home, the child's dying'. Emma refused, fearing assault if she left the house. Enoch grabbed Emma by the throat and dragged her into the back yard. Mrs Priest and her son tried desperately to part them, but not before Enoch stabbed Emma with a large knife, just above the heart. The knife broke, which probably saved Emma, but her ordeal would continue as Enoch now produced a loaded revolver. The struggle continued; Emma's screams alerted other neighbours, who rushed to help. Enoch shot at Emma but missed, two more shots were fired, one hitting the pantry door. Emma, badly injured, managed to break free and ran back into the house. Enoch took the opportunity to escape, his way back into the house being blocked.

Doctor Branday was called to attend to Emma, she had bruises, wounds and shot all over her head, face and body, and it was surprising that she was still alive. PC Donnellon (Cradley Heath) attended and ordered Emma be removed to Dudley Guest Hospital. She was taken there with the assistance of PC Richard Phillips (Dudley Wood) and on arrival was attended to by the House Surgeon and his team.

A search was immediately started for Enoch; thirteen police officers took part, led by Inspector Gibbs. One of the first places visited was Enoch's home, as officers feared for the safety of the children and Enoch's father. Three officers were detailed to guard the house, should Enoch return. PC Rivers (Primrose Hill) took up a position in the chain shop at the bottom of the garden. He waited patiently, watching as Solomon left the house and returned soon after with his other son, Reuben. After over an hour in position he heard a lock turning at the back of the house. He saw a man, who fitted the description of Enoch and, as the man disappeared into the house, Rivers ran from his hiding place towards the door. The officer had a narrow escape when a bullet came through the door, fired from Enoch's pistol.

Inside the house Solomon had told his son that the police were looking for him. Enoch said 'then I'll finish myself', put the revolver to his temple and shot himself. It is not clear whether this was the bullet that almost hit the officer. Doctor Belbin of Cradley was called, but was unable to save Enoch, as the bullet had passed straight through his head. This death occurred about three hours after the assault on Emma Cox.

These events however, were only the closing scenes of a day which had also seen the disappearance of twenty-five-year-old Caroline Pearson. The last confirmed sighting of her was shortly after 5.30 pm on Tuesday evening. Caroline lived with her mother and sister in Turners Lane, and worked at the Harris and Pearson Brickworks in Brettell Lane, Brierley Hill. She left work at 5.30 pm on Tuesday, with a friend Alice Westwood. Enoch Cox met the two women and took them to a local public house, the *Vine Inn*, where he bought beer for them all.

In the pub Enoch showed the women a revolver and bullets, and also a large clasp knife. This was later positively identified by Westwood when she was shown the knife used to stab Emma. The three left the public house and walked to an area called Sevendwellings, near The Delph; this was where Alice left Cox and Pearson. Sometime later, between nine and 9.30 pm, a couple fitting the description of the couple were seen drinking in the *Birchtree Cottage* public house at The Delph. One thing is certain, Caroline Pearson did not return home that night, and there were no further sightings of her alive.

The police were alerted and commenced a search for Caroline. Their task was made difficult because of the number of disused pit shafts in the area, as well as canal coppices and fields of rye. They had a large area to cover, over terrain that was difficult to search. The Police search was also hampered on Thursday by heavy rain.

Enoch Cox was buried at St Peter's, Cradley Parish Church, on Monday morning, 2 July. His remains were interred in an unmarked grave at the bottom of the churchyard, near the road. A large crowd had gathered early in the morning near the Cox house to watch the funeral procession. Police officers were on duty to ensure that the crowd behaved themselves, feelings were

The Birchtree Cottage *as it appears today. The original building in 1906 would not have looked much different. The space to the right would have led to one of the many paths through to Turners Lane and, importantly, Sevendwellings.* The authors

running high in the area and it was believed Emma Brooks might attend. She had been hounded away from the area when she had returned to collect her clothing and effects from the Cox house the morning after Enoch committed suicide.

Mourners included Solomon Cox, Enoch's brother Reuben, and an aunt and uncle; bearers were workmates, friends and neighbours. The coffin was not taken into the church, and after a short service at the graveside, appointed for use in the Diocese of Worcester for the burial of suicides, Enoch Cox was laid to rest.

Of Caroline Pearson nothing had been heard or seen, the police had good reason to fear that she was dead; this belief was based in part on information from Alice Westwood. She had described Enoch's unusual behaviour in the *Vine Inn*, where he had threatened to 'kill three before he would be contented'. The search continued for Caroline, but there were no sightings, and few leads to follow.

Part of the mystery of Caroline's disappearance would be solved on the evening of Tuesday, 10 July, exactly two weeks after she went missing. Some people walking a public footpath adjacent to a rye field, about 250 yards from the *Birchtree Cottage* public house smelt a sickening odour from a meadow belonging to Mr Sanderson. Being aware of the missing woman, they went to the *Birchtree Cottage* and told the brewer Harry Wilcox. Harry was the son of the licensee, Sarah Pitt Wilcox. Harry went straight to the spot with his dog, in company with Arthur Spencer and Lawrence Wooldridge. The dog went through the hedge and into the field, followed by Wilcox. About fifteen yards into the field the mystery of Caroline's location was solved. The dog had found the remains of a young woman.

The body later identified as Caroline lay on her back, her clothing in disarray, her corsets unfastened, her skirt pulled up and her shawl placed around her face and head. Caroline's basket lay about six feet from her body, her hat lay on her chest. The police had already searched this field, but found nothing. The rye-grass was at least three-feet-high and the heavy rain the night after she disappeared had flattened it, obliterating all signs that anyone had gone into the field. Superintendent James Johnson (Brierley Hill) and his officers quickly took charge at the scene. Doctor George P Gifford also attended and carried out a careful examination of the body *in situ*.

News of the grisly discovery quickly spread and a large crowd gathered near the field, forcing the police to divert resources to control them. Superintendent Johnson visited Harris and Pearson and they quickly made a rough coffin, used to transport

The area of the graveyard where Enoch Cox was laid to rest. The authors

The offices of Harris and Pearson, recently restored to their former glory. The authors

Caroline's remains to the *Eagle Inn*, Turners Lane, where the Coroners enquiry would take place.

On Wednesday afternoon Mr T Allan Stokes (South Staffordshire Coroner) held his inquest. A jury was sworn in; the foreman being Mr Dixon, Superintendent Johnson represented the police. One of the jurors, Mr Nesbitt, asked the Coroner if it was necessary for the jury to see the remains. The reply was 'You need not go very near; I cannot excuse you from going to see that there is something there to hold an inquest on'.

Identification of Caroline was made by her sister Annie; she identified her hat, basket and shawl, which she had seen Caroline wearing at 4.30 pm on the day she disappeared. Annie knew Enoch Cox; as he had visited the Pearson house with his daughter. Harry Wilcox gave evidence of finding the body, the location being only 250 yards from the public house where he lived and worked, and fifteen yards into the field from the footpath. Superintendent Johnson gave evidence of the position

Map showing the area where Caroline was found. Sevendwellings Bridge was the last confirmed sighting, the Eagle Inn *was where the inquest was held, and the* Birchtree Cottage *is where Enoch and Caroline were possibly drinking.* The authors

of the body and the manner in which her clothing was arranged. Her right hand was on her breast, he saw no signs of a struggle.

The next witness was Alice Rosannah Westwood. She stated she had been with the deceased all day at work; she also said she had last seen Caroline in company with Enoch Cox. Alice had known Enoch for some time, but she had very little to do with him. Alice was also shown the knife used to stab Emma, though now broken she recognised it as the one Enoch had shown Alice and Caroline when they were in the *Vine Inn*.

Doctor Gifford then gave his medical evidence. As a result of the time the body had lain undiscovered all the features had gone. The neck tissue was surprisingly well preserved, but the skin over the chest had disappeared in places. The heart and lungs were in an advanced state of decomposition. The weather in the two weeks had been very hot, speeding up the decay process. No visible evidence of stab or gunshot wounds was apparent, strangulation was also ruled out given the lack of injury on the neck. No marks had been found between the ribs to give any indication of wounds on the torso. There was nothing to indicate the cause of death and Caroline's heart and lungs were impossible to examine properly.

Having heard all the evidence Mr Stokes addressed the jury. His advice was that the only verdict they could return was one of 'found dead'; anything else was theory and speculation, as there was no means of establishing cause of death. It was no surprise when the jury returned a verdict of 'Found dead at Amblecote'.

Caroline Pearson was laid to rest on Thursday, 12 July at St Michael's Church, Brierley Hill. Her coffin bore a plate 'Caroline Pearson, died June 26 1906, aged twenty-five years'. A large crowd gathered, with about 1,500 outside the church-yard, there was an equally large gathering inside the church. The Reverend H H Dibben conducted the service at the graveside. He declared this was the saddest ministerial duty he had performed in his twenty-five years of being associated with the church.

With the laying to rest of Caroline an end was brought to a short, but sad episode in the life of two Black Country com-munities – Cradley and Brierley Hill. Many questions remained unanswered. What was the relationship between Enoch Cox

St Michael's Church, Brierley Hill. The authors

and Caroline Pearson? One can only speculate about how much the Pearson family knew about him. They knew he had a young daughter, for example. Enoch was most definitely one for the ladies; by all account he spent good money on clothes and his appearance. Another imponderable surrounds his marriage to Emma. Many Black Country men during this period would regularly beat their wives, often when they 'had the drink in them'. It was probably a greater ordeal for wives at the time to leave the matrimonial home. Divorce was not easy, accommodation not available, support for battered and abused wives probably non-existent.

What was Enoch Cox's state of mind during this period? His father said at his inquest that his son was 'most peculiar in his manner'. He certainly displayed odd behaviour on the day of the incidents and was probably not of sound mind. His threat to kill three that day almost came to pass. Emma Cox only survived after four weeks of constant care at Dudley Guest Hospital, and even then she left hospital with a disabled right arm, which hung as though paralysed.

The Reverend Dibben made pointed comments during the funeral of Caroline about living in 'tremendously wicked times'. He went on to say that sin was on the increase and pleaded for his listeners 'to take heed of this example of the sad end of that young woman'.

On the Sunday following the funeral Reverend Dibben delivered an address to a large congregation. He spoke of 'the awful tragedy that had taken place' that must have 'moved the hearts of Christian people to indignation'. He compared this incident to the Whitechapel Murders of some seventeen years previous. He also went on to make reference to the number of women to be found in public houses and said 'God help them when they had drunken mothers and drunken sisters in their house'. He concluded by highlighting the neglect of people who were not attending the House of God.

The map of the area helps show the geography; the first landmark mentioned is Harris and Pearson. At this time there were a number of brickworks etc. attributed to them. I am unable to identify exactly which one Caroline was met outside by Cox. The trio then went to the *Vine Inn*. There are a few pubs with that name that could possibly have been their destination. There is a *Vine Inn* at Lyde Green, near Cradley; however this is a long walk from Brierley Hill, and doesn't fit later events. There was another in Fenton Street in Brierley Hill, this fits as it is much closer. The trio then left the *Vine* and walked to Sevendwellings. This is on a direct line between Fenton Street and the *Birchtree Cottage*, and hence it is the pub I think they went to, this pub no longer exists.

The large expanse in the middle of the map consisted of mine workings, many disused, criss-crossed by footpaths; one would have been used by Caroline and Cox to get to the *Birchtree Cottage*. Finally, I believe Caroline went (or was taken) along the footpath that runs past Delph Colliery (marked on the map); one will see roughly where the 250 yard distance from the pub is found. The murder spot is now situated somewhere in the area that is Withymoor Village housing estate.

The verdict of 'found dead' was as a result of the lack of forensic evidence that would have assisted the jury. In a modern murder investigation techniques and equipment would have yielded much more evidence. This might have included the use of metal detectors to find evidence near the body, and DNA testing of the knife recovered following the attack on Emma Cox. The search for Caroline would have involved more professional search techniques, the use of helicopters with infra-red cameras, officers properly trained in search techniques and cadaver dogs are all weapons in the modern police armoury when dealing with missing persons. Caroline may not have been saved, but the investigation into her death might have returned a different verdict.

Bella in the Wych-Elm 1943

'Who put Bella in the Wych-Elm' was a question chalked on bridges, the walls of derelict houses and even on the pavements of the Black Country. The identity of the question's writer, as well as the identity of the body nicknamed 'Bella' is still a mystery over half a century later.

On 19 April 1943 four boys from Wollescote were bird-nesting in Hagley Woods on land owned by Viscount Cobham KCB. Their trek was a regular Sunday jaunt, known to them as 'The Clent Safari'. The boys took with them a collection of dogs – two lurchers, a cross bred fox terrier and a 'bush dog'. Bob Hart, Tom Willetts, Fred Payne and Bob Farmer were searching intently among trees and matted under-growth. They came across a Wych-elm; this seemed an ideal spot for a nest. To reach it the boys had to slide down a slope and one of them climbed up the tree. He looked inside the lichen-covered cavity. What was inside the hole of the tree was not a bird's nest, something white gleamed in the gloom. The boys had found a skull.

Initially the boys speculated about the origin of the skull, was it a dog, or a ferret, but one of them, Tom Willetts, the youngest of the group, was certain that what he had seen was a human skull. The boys made their way home, reluctant to tell anyone of their find as they knew they had been trespassing. On the way they met Fred's elder brother Donald, who was at first sceptical about their find. Donald went back to the tree with the boys, and was convinced the boys were correct; a human skull was in the tree.

Tom Willett's father was informed and he contacted his local Police Sergeant, Charles Lambourne, stationed at Cradley Heath. He immediately telephoned Sergeant Richard Skerratt in charge at Clent, and arranged to meet him, with the boys, in Hagley Wood. Other police officers were summoned to attend the scene, PC Jack Pound from Hagley and Sergeant Jack Wheeler (of the motor patrol). The boys pointed out the relevant tree, and one look inside by the experienced officers was enough to convince the police that the tree contained a human skull.

Police activity in the case, by modern standard, was slow, but communications systems were not as advanced as they are today. Sergeant Skerratt returned to his station and telephoned Superintendent Holyhead, at Police Headquarters in Stourbridge. He in turn contacted the CID based at Hindlip Hall, Worcester. The subsequent investigation was handled by Detective Superintendent Knight, assisted by Detective Inspector Thomas Williams, who quickly attended the scene. The team were accompanied by Professor Jim Webster from the West Midlands Forensic Science Laboratory.

The area around the elm was cordoned off and photographed. It was then necessary to enlarge the tree cavity for a more thorough investigation of the interior. Jack Pound had the necessary skills as he was an ex-lumberman; and he cut a large wedge-shape hole into the tree. The skull was examined by Professor Webster who forced open the jaws. The mouth was tightly stuffed with cotton material and Webster immediately pronounced the case to be murder. This prognosis is more than likely correct, however it is possible that the evidence of suffocation may have been tainted by the boys when they found the skull. The search continued, other parts of the skeleton were found, located in a sitting position, the skull having toppled off. A closer examination of the skull revealed strands of hair on the side of the cranium that had been in contact with the ground.

A thorough search of the woodland around the wych-elm was now conducted. This included sieving the earth in the elm for forensic evidence. By widening the search an almost complete skeleton was pieced together. Some bones were found several yards away, possibly torn from the body by animals and carried away by them. Two items of interest found inside the cavity were one of a pair of blue crepe-soled woman's shoes, the other was found nearby in the wood, and a cheap gold wedding ring

BODY WAS FOUND HERE

Picture of the tree where Bella was found, taken some years after the discovery. Courtesy of Wolverhampton *Express and Star*

with the words 'rolled gold' stamped on the inside. The search was again widened and assistance came from members of the Home Guard, Scouts and ARP wardens who all participated in a methodical search in ever-widening circles around the elm.

A more scientific approach was to reveal a few facts about the victim. Professor Webster confirmed the skeleton was that of a woman, aged about thirty-five. She had been five-feet tall and had given birth to one child; he also deduced she had not been a manual worker. Her hair was 'mousey' in colour, and a tooth had been extracted in the year prior to her death. Death had occurred between one and four years prior to her discovery, and he narrowed this down further to about eighteen months. More clues were unusual front teeth; her incisor teeth were crossed in a most singular manner. It was most likely that she had been pushed into the tree while still warm, increasing the likelihood that she was killed at or near the tree.

Given the possible date of death of about eighteen months Sergeant Skerratt remembered an incident in Hagley Wood that he and PC Pound had attended. Screams had been heard during the night, near the location of the wych-elm. The officers had made a thorough search of the wood, but with no trace of anything untoward. It was thought likely that the sound was the scream of a vixen, often mistaken for a human voice. At around the suggested time of death another event was remembered. An encampment of gypsies had been in the area; they had often engaged in noisy quarrels amongst each other. The gypsies were traced and once again nothing came from the enquiry.

Slogans then began to appear on walls in Blackheath, Halesowen and Netherton – 'Who put Bella in the Wych-Elm?' Other variants used the name 'Luebella' and 'Hagley Wood Bella'. Analysis of the handwriting revealed no clues. Enquires were made with anyone named Bella, Isobella and Luebella – all known women with those names were traced and confirmed alive and well.

With the assistance of Lord Cobham's woodsman I recently visited the site of the find. No trace remains of the tree stump, the wych-elm falling prey to Dutch elm disease, which has robbed this country of all its elm trees. The location is about thirty yards from an un-classified road that is only used by a few vehicles and visitors to the Clent Hills.

Many theories developed, and national interest in the case was great. A nearby local public-house was the *Gypsy's Tent*, (now a restaurant of the Beefeater chain and re-named the *Badgers Sett*), it was here that searchers often adjourned for refreshment, and where theories on the case were discussed. Speculation from local PC Harry Pound was that the offender was a soldier in the army, and probably away at war.

Another suggested that 'Bella' was the victim of a ritual witchcraft murder (in folklore the wych-elm was the home of witches and woodland spirits). A further theory speculated that she was an itinerant, possibly a gypsy or fugitive from city bombing, even a casualty of war – made homeless, possibly her husband and child dead, which led to her not being reported missing. Others held the belief that the killer was a local man who carefully chose the spot to dispose of the body of his victim. A victim of domestic violence was also considered.

Further theories have since been aired about 'Bella', particularly in the local press, being a 'casualty of war', another that 'Bella' was a spy, sent by Germany in 1941 to report back the location of munitions factories for the Luftwaffe. She was believed to be Dutch, and was killed by two other members of the ring when it was found out that she knew too much about

Example of the graffiti that appeared shortly after the discovery of Bella. Courtesy of Wolverhampton *Express and Star*

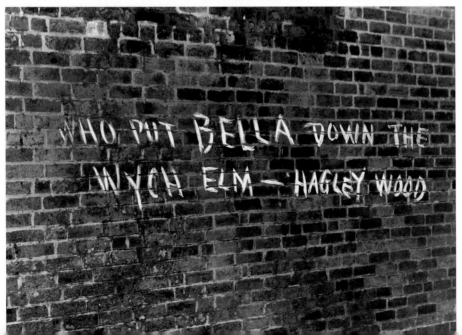

members of the ring. Yet another put forward the possibility she may have been a German astronomer who had escaped from one of Hitler's purges. Yet another suggested the death may have been suicide and quoted Sir Sidney Smith, Professor of Forensic Medicine at Edinburgh University.

On the Wednesday following the discovery, at Stourbridge, an inquest was held by Mr F P Evers (Coroner for North Worcestershire). The eight-man jury returned a verdict of 'murder by some person or persons unknown'. The murder was to make news through-out the country, despite the Second World War being foremost in everyone's mind.

Evidence was given of the clothing worn, namely a dark blue and light khaki or mustard-coloured striped cardigan. She also wore a light khaki or mustard-coloured woollen skirt, a peach taffeta rayon underskirt, navy blue interlock knickers, corsets and blue crepe-soled shoes. The general quality of the clothing was poor.

The inquest also heard from Robert Hart, aged nineteen, of Pearson Street, Wollescote. It was he who went to the tree stump and found the skull and bones. One of the others hooked the skull out with a stick. Having examined it they pushed it back in as near to its former position as possible.

Sergeant Skerratt stated that the diameter of the aperture at its widest point was about twenty-four inches, and at the narrowest seventeen inches. From the base of the hollow, which was four-feet-seven-inches across, to the top of the shaft was about three feet. The tree was located about thirty-five yards from Hagley Wood Lane.

Professor Webster re-constructed the skeleton, allowing him to work out age and height. He found no disease, or indication of violence to the bones. When questioned about the possibility of suicide Professor Webster ruled this out, saying he could not imagine anyone being able to climb into the trunk without considerable damage and tearing, he also ruled out accident. He concluded by saying he believed the body was placed inside before rigor mortis had set in. This presumption was based on the fact that the body was in a seated position inside the tree.

Any murder enquiry begins with the scene and what evidence can be yielded. It is a known fact that most murder victims know their killer. Therefore, it becomes crucial to quickly identify the victim. In the case of 'Bella' there were few primary clues that would assist the police with identification of the victim.

The crepe shoes found with the skeleton were an important line of enquiry to be followed. This was assigned to Detective Inspector Williams to expedite. They were traced to a Northampton manufacturer, and Williams would work to try and trace the purchaser of every pair sold. Eventually all but six pairs were eliminated, all sold at a Black Country market with no clue to the identity of the purchaser. The unusual structure of Bella's teeth would lead to a nationwide investigation whereby almost every dentist in the country was contacted. The investigators were confident that this line of enquiry would bear fruit. However, this would not be the case, and progress became very slow. The possibility that Bella was not British became higher because of this.

In the 1970s the *Black Country Bugle*, then a monthly local newspaper, took up the investigation. One of the areas they focused on was the shoes. Mr Cogzell, who ran a boot and shoe repair shop in Lye, claimed he could identify the shoes as a pair he had seen being repaired in a shop, in Lye, in 1933. He had seen the shoes on a television programme in 1970, by Professor Webster. Arrangements were made for Mr Cogzell to view the shoes at Birmingham University. However, when shown the shoes he was adamant that the shoes he was handling were not the same as the ones shown on television, another enquiry ended in a dead end. There were also letters to the *Bugle*, seemingly from someone with knowledge of the case. One came from Canada and alluded to the wartime spy theory.

Sir Sidney Smith wrote of a case in his memoirs *Mostly Murder* of the case of a woman found dead in her bedroom. Her maid had been unable to gain access to the room; the doctor attended and broke down the door. The woman was dead in bed and partly covering her mouth was a scarf, tied at the back. On closer examination there was a small handkerchief, tightly pushed into the back of her throat. All the signs pointed to murder, but the woman was suffering severe depression, and had previously threatened suicide, self strangulation had been attempted previously, always in front of witnesses. The verdict was one of suicide. This possibility is highly unlikely in the case of Bella. The lack of evidence of anything but a clean entry into the tree, there was nothing holding the material inside the mouth, which was a feature in the Sydney Smith case. I do not believe Bella committed suicide.

The mystery has also inspired Simon Holt, who was in the 1980s an associate composer with the City of Birmingham Symphony Orchestra. He wrote a music-theatre piece about the murder in 2002 and tells the story through the eyes of an elderly man who witnessed the killing but did not come forward.

In the twenty-first century new technologies are available to investigators. DNA, for example, could have led to a positive identification, but only if 'Bella' had previously come to the notice of the police, and was on their database. DNA could also assist if blood relatives were traced, as comparing their DNA to that of the deceased can lead to positive identification. Low-count DNA means that today much smaller DNA samples from the victim could have been used, the hair found attached to the skull, for example.

The sharing of information on people reported missing is also now well established between police forces both in Britain and across the rest of the world. Outside agencies, such as the Salvation Army also play a part in tracing missing persons. The media also plays a greater part in cases such as this, television and the Internet could easily be used to publicise the case. Other scientific methods, such as a forensic re-construction of 'Bella's' skull would have given police yet another avenue of investigation.

Bella's clothing suggests she came from the Black Country, or had spent some time there. The fact she was not thought to be a manual worker and her poor clothing suggests possibly a refugee. The manner of her death is not certain, asphyxiation seems favourite, but the evidence is not conclusive. There is no evidence to support or discount poisoning or drugs, and maybe she was alive, but unconscious when placed into the tree. There were no marks that indicated a struggle at the tree or inside, no bark or debris under the fingernails was mentioned, if they were found.

A more modern example of the graffiti that has appeared featuring Bella, from a monument about one mile from the site. The authors

The graffiti is also puzzling, why did it appear? Was the originator involved in the killing, or someone who read of the case, which was widely publicised? Was the name used to cast a smoke screen over the investigation, certainly the police, with few other clues, seized on the possibility? The name used is also unusual; 'Bella' itself is a shortened version of a number of names, possibly indicating the originator knew the victim personally. If someone picked the name at random why not choose a much more common name to make enquiries more difficult.

These questions are mere speculation. It is too late, and there is too little material to allow a modern-day 'cold case' review. No witness to the murder has ever been found, and nature put paid to most meaningful forensic leads. The Second World War also meant plenty of people moved around the region – military and other support staff, factory workers, refugees, prisoners of war, even spies who undoubtedly operated in the area, given the significance of the industrial heartland to the war effort. We will never identify Bella after all this time, nor will we trace her killers. Interest will continue in the case, more theories and spins on current theories will continue to surface as long as people remember the case.

Conclusion

The above sixteen cases demonstrate that over a period of six centuries, foul deeds and suspicious deaths have never been absent in and around the Black Country. Whilst certain crimes such as internet or credit-card fraud are very much of their time, crimes such as murder have occurred since the human race first evolved.

We have tried to give a flavour of the numerous crimes that have taken place in and around the Black Country and which are recorded in a wide variety of sources. Researching the crimes has made us realise the tremendous steps in both jurisprudence and detection that have been made within the last hundred years or so. No longer is the defendant banned from giving evidence on oath; or is (s)he unable to obtain a qualified legal defence counsel for want of funds. Similarly, several of the foul deeds and suspicious deaths detailed in this book would undoubtedly have been solved had they occurred today – the plethora of forensic tests from fingerprinting, blood-sampling and DNA 'fingerprinting' that have been developed throughout the twentieth century up to the present-day would have made our mediaeval, Georgian, Victorian and Edwardian police officers' lives much easier.

However, it is equally apparent that whilst judicial and detective methods may have changed over the centuries, the motives for the foul deeds and murders detailed in the book have not. Humans have remained fundamentally unaltered: greed, jealousy and cruelty are unfortunately very much still part of mankind's nature.

Researching the cases, it has been hard not to become involved with the lives of the participants in each of the cases. It is fairly straightforward to establish the how, what, where, and when of the facts surrounding each of the cases. It is far more difficult, if not impossible, to detect the motives behind the carrying out of many of the foul deeds described in the book.

Some of the cases evince pity and horror, others a degree of humour and even admiration for an audacious rogue.

We hope that readers have experienced at least some of these feelings during their perusal of the book and that their interest in our fascinating and largely well-documented criminal justice history has been stimulated.

Staffordshire Advertiser, *9 March 1839, listing trials to be held at the forthcoming Staffordshire Assizes. The trials listed include that of Susannah Perry for the murder of her husband (see pp. 65–70).* Authors' collection

STAFFORDSHIRE ASSIZES.

The Commission of Assize for this county will be opened on Monday next. At present, it is doubtful whether the learned Judges (Mr. Justice Patteson and Mr. Justice Erskine) will attend divine service after the opening of the commission on Monday, or on Tuesday morning; but it will be well for Grand and Petty Jurymen, and others who have business at the Assizes, to be in readiness by nine o'clock on Tuesday morning, as it is not improbable that business may commence in both courts at that time—the Assizes at Worcester being likely to terminate on Saturday night, at the latest.

Mr. Alderman Copeland, M.P., is expected to officiate for Wm. Moore, Esq., the High Sheriff, who will not be able to attend in person, on account of a recent domestic bereavement.

Of the extent of the business at *Nisi Prius,* no opinion can at present be formed.

The number of prisoners for trial yesterday was forty-eight; and, from the following abstract of the calendar, it will be seen that some of the offences are of a very serious nature :—

Murder—Susannah Perry, (aged 39.)

Burglary, Arson, and Attempt to Murder—Joseph Newberry, (aged 21,) Joseph Taylor, (aged 18.)

Rape—Henry Thomas, (aged 38.)

Bestiality—John James, (aged 24.)

Uttering Forged Notes—William Miles, (aged 19.)

Manslaughter—Laurence Hill, (aged 56,) George Grove, (30,) George Terry, (22,) Benjamin Terry, (20,) John Hunt, (24,) James Hodgkiss, (22,) and Daniel Betts, (23.)

Cutting and Stabbing.—Thomas Finlow, (aged 22,) Abraham Ball, Eliza Fairfield, (25,) John Hollins, (18.)

Burglary.—Joseph Grattage, (aged 21,) James Bramwell, (19,) Thos. Bramwell, (19,) John Malbon, (27,) Thomas Rushton, (38,) Joseph Whieldon, (22.)

Sheep Stealing.—Archibald McCallum, (58,) Langam Dodd, (40,) Ralph Foster, (28.)

Cow Stealing.—John Pace, (25.)

Horse Stealing.—Thomas Rushton, (18,) John Downing, (30,) William Stokes.

Highway Robbery.—John Bromley, (19,) James Humphreys, (32,) James Blakemore, 22,) Elizabeth Adams, (23,) Charles Shipley, (17,) William Gordon, (19.)

Night Poaching.—James Watson, (21,) John Salt, (22,) Joseph Gosling, (25.)

Perjury.—James Bennett, (23.)

Bigamy.—William Blower, (36.)

Larceny.—William Chesters, (16,) John Holland, (28,) Daniel Lines, (27,) William Fox, (17,) Benjamin Lashford, David Mackintyre, and William Downing.

Uttering base Coin.—Richard Edwards.

Further Reading

Crime and Punishment

Abbott, Geoffrey, William Calcraft: Executioner Extraordinaire (Verulam Publishing, 2004).

Barrett, A. and C. Harrison, *Crime and Punishment in England* (UCL Press, 1999).

Evans, Stewart P., *Executioner: The Chronicles of James Berry, Victorian Hangman* (Sutton Publishing, 2005).

Gatrell, V. A. C., *The Hanging Tree: Execution and the English People 1770–1868* (OUP Paperbacks, 1996).

Hawkings, David T., *Criminal Ancestors: A Guide to Historical Criminal Records in England and Wales* (Sutton Publishing, 1996).

Hay, D., and F. Snyder (Eds.), *Policy and Prosecution in Britain, 1750–1850* (OUP, 1989).

Justice

Beattie, J. M., *Crime and the Courts in England 1660–1800* (OUP, 1986).

Eastwood, David, *Government and Community in the English Provinces 1700–1870* (Macmillan, 1997).

Landau, Norma (Ed.), *Law, Crime and English Society 1660–1830* (CUP, 2002).

Parker, H., M. Sumner, and G. Jarvis, *Unmasking the Magistrates* (Open University Press, 1989).

Skyrme, Sir T., *History of the Justices of the Peace* (Barry Rose Publishing, 1994).

Policing

Emsley, Clive, *Crime and Society in England 1750–1900*, 3rd edition (Longman, 2004).

Emsley, Clive, *The English Police: A Political and Social History*, 2nd edition (Longman, 1996).

Philips, David, and Robert Storch, *Policing Provincial England 1829–1856: the politics of reform* (Leicester University Press, 1999).

Rawlings, Philip, *Policing: A short history* (Willan Press, 2002).

Local interest

Cockin, Tim, *The Staffordshire Encyclopaedia* (Malthouse Press, 2000).

Conan Doyle, Sir Arthur, *The Story of Mr George Edalji* (Grey House Books, 1985).

Cox, David, *The Dunsley Murder of 1812: A Study in Early Nineteenth-Century Crime Detection, Justice and Punishment* (Dulston Press, 2003).

Cox, David, and Barry Godfrey (Eds.), *Cinderellas and Packhorses: A History of the Shropshire Magistracy* (Logaston Press, 2005).

Lethbridge, J., *Murder in the Midlands: Notable Trials of the Nineteenth Century* (Robert Hale, 1989).

Philips, David, *Crime and Authority in Victorian England: The Black Country, 1835–60* (Croom Helm, 1977).

The Blackcountryman, the quarterly journal of the Black Country Society, contains a wide variety of crime-related articles published during its thirty-eight year existence. The first ten volumes containing forty issues of the magazine are available on a CD-ROM (See www.blackcountrysociety.co.uk for more details).

Index